# ARCHITECTURAL SUPERVISION
## ON SITE

# ARCHITECTURAL SUPERVISION ON SITE

## A. A. MACFARLANE

*Chartered Architect and Town Planning Consultant*
*Associate of the Royal Institute of British Architects*
*Member of the Royal Town Planning Institute*

APPLIED SCIENCE PUBLISHERS LTD

LONDON

APPLIED SCIENCE PUBLISHERS LTD
RIPPLE ROAD, BARKING, ESSEX, ENGLAND

ISBN: 0 85334 574 0

WITH 24 ILLUSTRATIONS

Printed in Great Britain by Galliard (Printers) Limited, Great Yarmouth, Norfolk, England.

# Contents

# CHAPTER 1

# *Introduction*

An architect engaged to give 'normal service' as defined in the RIBA *Conditions of Engagement* is required to inspect work on site during the progress of the building contract, and he is also bound to do this by the terms of the *Standard Form of Contract* issued by the Joint Contracts Tribunal. The architect for the purpose of inspections may be anyone the named architect may depute to carry out inspections on his behalf, despite the omission from the Form of provision for naming anyone to act in his stead. The contractor must permit the named architect 'and his representative' to inspect works on site and in workshops, which implies they visit in consort. The representative is not required to have any technical knowledge yet the contractor is apparently not able to object to visits by an unsatisfactory representative. It must be assumed that the architect will only appoint as his representative one having the technical and administrative qualities suitable for the stage of the contract. Obviously, however, the representative ought to be one permitted to sign orders on behalf of the architect and be for contract purposes the architect *pro tem* and is to be so understood in the following chapters.

Neither the *Conditions of Engagement* nor the *Form of Contract* states precisely what is meant by 'inspect' but it is evident that this means looking at work already done, including preliminary work for stages of work to follow. Merely to look at what has been done is scarcely sufficient for the conscientious exercise of his function in assisting the smooth progress of the contract. He should also bear in mind future operations which may have a bearing on (*a*) work being inspected and (*b*) work likely to be done before his next visit.

The number of inspections to be made is nowhere set down. The requirement that the architect shall give 'sufficient attention' to the works is extremely vague. It may be affected by travelling distance,

1

rate of progress, unforeseeable crises and availability of time and staff. In addition, complexity of the job, contractor's integrity and ability to interpret the architect's intentions are other factors.

As no rule has been fixed, each contract must be considered separately and the spacing of the inspections arranged accordingly. While regularly spaced inspections are customary they have both good and bad points. In favour is the knowledge of the contractor that he must have his query list ready by these days and can arrange specialist subcontractors' representatives to be available, while prompting him to complete stages of work as forecast at the previous inspection and listing deliveries made of special items and future delivery dates promised. An objection is the loss of the 'surprise' factor in which the architect appears unexpectedly, possibly at some peculiarly vital stage such as excavation for foundations in variable clay or placing of steel reinforcement where speed may have taken precedence over accuracy. There may also be visits at the contractor's request where problems arise, such as brick pier dimensions to be varied due to facing bricks as delivered being undersized, or specialists' items which raise procedural or protection problems involving possible delays or additional costs.

Where an architect or assistant architect is on site at all times, the need for visits by the nominated architect is clearly less necessary and could be held to be superfluous, but this runs the risk of breakdown in communication with the design and administration office. This in turn makes the site architect extremely vulnerable.

The importance of conscientious inspection of work cannot be over-emphasised. A well-prepared contract smoothly administered and with decisions taken by the architect in good time should reduce the number of special visits, given an equally good contractor working in times of adequate supplies of materials, plant and labour, but this does not excuse the architect from making quite sure at fairly frequent intervals with his own eyes, or at least those of his capable representative, that the contract is going as intended. He is paid to inspect, and his client has the right to require him to know how well the contract is progressing, and not just from letters from the builder or records of telephone conversations. In a contract in which muddle, ineptitude and lack of skill are ever-present on site, it is not an acceptable excuse by the architect that he did not visit the site at abnormally frequent intervals because such supervision would have cost him more in time than the proportion of his fee allowed. This may be the subject of a complaint but not of a claim for additional fees, except possibly where the client has insisted on nominating the contractor against the architect's wishes. Even so any claim for additional fees would be ill-advised.

The economics of site visits are largely centred on the efficiency of the inspection. To be efficient the architect must understand all that he sees, interpreting small evidences correctly, or, if he is unable to do this, inquiring what these mean; *e.g.* in noting in a reveal of a window opening in a cavity wall that no vertical DPC can be seen to separate the two skins and asking the builder how this comes about. To realise at an inspection that a defect had been overlooked at a previous visit is an admission of inefficiency, yet not an admission to be silenced, for professional integrity requires the admission to be made and the defect righted or overcome. Power of observation must be developed in the casual glance as in close study, and the antecedents of the work done must be understood at the same time as evaluation for future stages is assessed. Inspections are concerned with work done in all trades to the end of the contract, in so far as decisions can be made.

Architects are taught nothing of job management from the con-tractor's point of view. The economical use of plant and choice of types are beyond him and are not considered to be in his province, yet there should be an understanding of the contractor's problems. Economic progress of a contract on site may rely on a certain sequence of works which the architect had not contemplated, yet unless the terms of the contract have been exceptionally varied it is not in the architect's power to dictate to the contractor how some sequences of work shall be done, so long as no delay or weakness may result from the contractor's sequence. There may be opposing views here, the contractor insisting that only good can result from accepting his sequence. The architect then has to decide whether to allow the contractor to do the job his way, writing to say he disagrees but putting the onus on the contractor for unsatisfactory results, or taking the extreme step of stopping the contract which he should only do after consulting the client and all the 'authorities' he can think of. The contractor would not normally risk this stage being reached, and so would be likely to re-arrange the sequence to one acceptable to the architect and to record his objection to the archi-tect's interference coupled with reluctant agreement to the change. He might also wish to record that a claim or claims will be made in due course for extra costs and loss of profits. This situation could arise where the use of the building or site was in some way unusual and known only to the client and the architect.

The architect and contractor in dispute have their rights for future action set out in the *Form of Contract*, but every avenue to avoid a head-on clash should be examined while preserving dignity and, maybe in borderline cases, an escape route. A client will not readily accept termination of a contract, which will almost certainly result in delay and enhanced and ancillary costs, unless he is satisfied that his architect has gone as far as reasonable to keep the contract operative without more detrimental effects on the client's pocket. The situation that arises when a private architect is commissioned by an elected body can be particularly difficult, for garbled information inimical to the architect's case in the dispute quickly circulates.

The architect's representative finding himself in dispute with a builder is in a much more difficult situation, and so he must be even more careful to record the facts of the situation unambiguously and report fully to the architect without delay. Only in cases of danger to the public or to other buildings should a representative tell the contractor to stop work, and even then probably only on that section which is the subject of dispute. He would certainly be well advised to report by telephone to the architect so that the latter should issue the order. This is not cowardice on the part of the representative: it enables the architect to look at the problem as the person named in the contract, and maybe by virtue of longer or different experience and higher contact with the contractors, he may find at least a temporary solution to the dispute.

The architect must understand the meanings and purposes of the *Standard Form of Contract*, of which there are editions for public authority use as well as private contracts (which may include public companies) with or without quantities. Some public bodies have their own forms of contract which they insist on using and which must therefore be digested by the architect. Interpretation and case law really require study assisted by commentaries on contract which are continually being supplemented by law reports setting precedents and slanting previous decisions in new directions. The contract allows the contractor to query the right of an architect to order certain actions and requires an architect to do certain things at certain times. Curiously enough the contract does not say what happens when an architect fails to do what he ought to do, as for example failing to send the contractor a schedule of defects within 14 days following the end of the defects liability period.

No architect can be expected to know all the peculiar techniques of the growing number of building trades. He ought to have a fairly clear understanding of the traditional trades like strip foundations, brickwork and carpentry, but even these will occasionally have him in doubt, *e.g.* bearing capacity of subsoil, bond of solid wall to cavity wall and skew jointing of beams. He has to be diffident about condemning work until he is sure he understands what he sees, and even so a question or two may show that what he would have liked to see could not have been carried out, such as the placing of a water-stop in a concrete slab joint which on site looks so remarkably different from what is shown in the advertisements. He cannot be an expert in all trades or always be aware of changes in these trades in which he thinks himself well-informed. He has to rely on his under-standing of principles when he finds, for instance, that a vapour barrier is badly perforated or that incompatible materials are being mixed. If his ideas of principles are being abused it may be because he is unaware that some scientific development has been seized on by a specialist to make the job better or quicker and can only learn of this by asking the fixer why well-tried principles are being broken. It falls then to the architect to do a little research, probably by going to the specialist as his source.

This situation is happening at frequent intervals yet it is not always the architect who is ignorant. All professional journals carry advertise-ment pages which are mines of valuable information, even when only proclaiming that some development has been achieved—please send for details. The conscientious architect studies advertisement pages and technical literature and assesses values, perhaps being aided by inquiries. The architect is then probably better informed than many tradesmen on the site, finding in some work that neither the contractor nor his tradesman really understands the uses of new materials. This however may not be the end of the story, for it may be learned that there are practical objections to carrying out the architect's wishes, such as difficulty in getting a special adhesive in small quantities, its short pot-life or its ineffectiveness in cold weather. It then falls to someone to find an alternative acceptable to all, including the contractor, the architect or the merchant. Dictation achieves few victories.

It is customary and often obligatory to state in specifications and descriptions in Bills of Quantities that materials must conform to certain British Standards and work must be done in accordance with certain Codes of Practice. Where materials or devices carry the 'kite' mark no problems arise, except that since that mark was applied the standard may have appeared in a new edition or may even have been superseded. Where good practice is concerned, most codes largely confirm common practice, but obscurities can be found if one searches. Architects could, in their specifications or in the bills of quantities, require the contractor always to have on site a copy of the BS Handbook No. 3 and a copy of each Code of Practice which is applicable. Handbook No. 3 contains specifications only in abbreviated form and not infrequently leaves out the vital information required. To require the contractor to have on site a copy of every up-to-date issue of the standards that might be required for reference is surely too much.

There are also occasions where an item is different from and functions better than anything contemplated in a British Standard yet bears no kite mark. The architect is in a dilemma but it is not an uncommon situation and he must take a great deal on trust because he cannot always be sure. On being offered a lock he may note that its springbolt is made of plastics and not brass which he is used to: should he therefore condemn it although it is made by a reputable company and is otherwise good? More likely he will give provisional approval then find out from the makers or a merchant he knows well how long this kind of springbolt has been in use and what sort of warranty it carries. Only if the answers are suspect should he refuse to accept it—and maybe not then even if the lock is to be used on a small number of unimportant doors.

Much valuable knowledge on site matters and materials is circulated more so to architects than to site staff, including Building Research Establishment Digests, Department of the Environment Advisory Leaflets and trade association proceedings. Site inspections provide the opportunity to apply the information in these, the problem being, of course, to remember the data and know how to apply them when speaking to people with a life-time of experience in their own trades. When pitchfibre drain pipes first came on the UK market they were used indiscriminately without much thought of what could go wrong, being regarded as foolproof. Even now the degree of care proper to bedding and backfilling is often not followed or its objects understood. On the other hand, trade association meetings aimed at site staff may result in more practical applications of developments than the architect can glean from the printed word.

The assistant architect inspecting on behalf of the nominated architect is generally accepted by the contractor as having authority to approve, disapprove or vary requirements as agent for the architect. How far this authority should go must depend on the knowledge of the assistant on practical building, design and administration. An inexperienced assistant straight out of college would not be long on site without getting out of his depth and so ought to act only as a reporter to the architect, noting the states of the various trades and any peculiarities, but avoiding conclusions which the architect can reach on the basis of the assistant's report. Strictly, of course, this kind of visit scarcely satisfies the *Conditions of Engagement,* the assistant not being fledged while the architect is evading his real personal professional duty. When assistants entered the profession as pupils or improver/draughtsmen they learned site supervision by accompanying the job architect and no one felt discomfited.

Today the detachment of training from practice and site works exposes the graduate to the humiliation of knowing less about every trade than the young apprentices in these trades. This situation has to be accepted initially, so that the more site inspections the assistant can make along with the maximum reading of the technical literature that is available to architects the less risk he runs of making the more ludicrous misinterpretations of what he sees on the jobs or of making impractical recommendations like adding gypsum plaster to cement mortar to get it to harden quickly or flash to a copper roof with high-purity aluminium.

There are occasions when there are two ways of achieving much the same end, the contractor preferring one and the architect the other. It was the practice years ago to use slates as VDPC stuck with mortar to reveals of openings in walls as an alternative to bituminous felt between the outer and returned inner skins. The former is a stiffer, stronger job, the skins being bonded together, and where heavy lintels are to be supported this may be preferred. The architect however may argue that slate is not vapour-proof and, since its thermal insulation value when plastered over is very low, condensation on the reveals would be an everlasting trouble in winter. This would not be so acute where the skins are separated by the bituminous DPC. The architect or assistant may then be invited to solve the problem of the support for the lintel bearing only on the inner skin of questionable stability.

Inspecting work in progress inevitably leaves some work un-inspected: that is obvious and the larger the job the more obvious. There is the risk that the more smoothly a contract runs, the more tidy the site and orderly the stacks of materials the more the architect may be lulled into a sense of well-being with the temptation to take much for granted. This may be justified, a well-managed site implying a knowledgeable contractor's staff that is unwilling to have to do any operation twice through the architect condemning it the first time. Site visits can be illuminating, helpful and sociable—sitting in the site agent's office drinking tea while the problems of labour and deliveries are discussed along with study of detail drawings, the architect being convinced that this earnest attention to minutiae proves the excellence of the contractor—but it is not strictly an 'inspection'. These meetings are desirable and probably necessary, but not at the expense of thorough inspection of the site works. It is one of the ways supervision costs escalate. The site agent or his deputy can talk about many problems whilst accompanying the architect around the site with much saving in time.

One of the threats to professional practice is the increasing inclina-tion of clients to find fault with their architects to the extent of claiming negligence in design, administration and supervision. The wise architect ensures that every step in the contract from initial instructions to final account is adequately recorded. He has to be able to produce evidence, perhaps in the law courts, that he has carried out his duties conscientiously. Records of site inspections are the least common in an architect's documentation, yet this is where many architects have met trouble from clients. If a house foundation settles at one corner, can the architect produce a report of an inspec-tion of the excavation for foundations which incidentally records that the contractor was instructed to deepen the foundation at that point because there was a 'soft' spot—and a copy of a confirmation of the verbal instruction to the contractor? This record would not necessarily absolve the architect, but at least he has a good point in his favour. The job file should record all meetings and subjects discussed, important telephone conversations and names of approved materials —in fact it should be a diary of the contract.

The contract requires the architect to confirm verbal instructions within seven days (unless the contractor confirms or unless the instruction is carried out and confirmed by the architect prior to final certificate). This means one week, not seven working days, so allowing for a 5-day week and postal delays when the site is remote from the architect's office this allowance is tight. The architect could take advantage of the clause permitting the contractor to confirm in the same period but this is not a creditable device and does not avoid misunderstanding. The only system that really works, and then only when the assistant making the inspection has authority to sign on the architect's behalf, is to use a site instruction book having top copy and three carbon copies: top sheet for contractor, first carbon copy for quantity surveyor, second copy for either the clerk of works or office file, and the last copy retained in the book, all headed by the job name, job number, date of order and number of order (if practicable), name of contractor, name of subcontractor or trader as applicable, signature of giver of order (legible) and name of architect. This kind of book is not readily available, but a triplicate book is a passable substitute, albeit deficient. A duplicate book is a poor alternative because the page numbering is wrong, but this can be overcome by converting it into a quadruplicate book. At any rate some form of site order book really is essential, especially when the architect wants his instruction to take effect immediately. The point here is that the contractor need not take action until confirmation is received from the architect up to a week later. The architect can follow up the site orders with periodic instruction orders, either repeating the wording of the site orders or quoting dates and subjects. The wording of site orders should preferably be agreed with the contractor in case there are ambiguities, such as an instruction to use scrim on plaster board joints when this could mean either paper or cotton scrim, or an instruction to *plaster* a wall when the architect meant to *render* it. The assistant giving a site order to be confirmed by the architect is faced with the risk that the architect may not agree with him, as when an assistant tells the contractor to tusk-tenon a joist to a trimmer when the architect thinks a joist hanger would have been equally effective. There are alternative ways of doing most jobs, and the architect with the wider and longer experience should be the one to know of these, so differences like this are bound to happen. In this case the architect ought not to vary the site order and substitute his own solution because that is undermining the authority he has placed on his assistant. Yet there will certainly be cases where he must, and the reasons should be explained to his assistant.

Problems frequently arise on site because drawings cannot be adequately detailed. At the inspection, the architect is usually presented with a list of queries about small matters on the drawings which the contractor expects him to settle on the spot. This can be dangerous, for time is often needed for study in the office. The architect who prepares his own drawings or at least supervises them can with some assurance arrive at most of the answers. An assistant who has not prepared all the drawings is in a dangerous spot. A question may seem quite innocent: 'can't we move this soil stack to the next brick pier to avoid having a bend sitting on top of a column base?' The answer could be 'I don't see why not—it would be a shorter run, too'; but on studying the heating drawings one might find that the stack was deliberately placed there to allow heating flow and return pipes to rise/drop at the suggested nearby pier without fouling something else. Or perhaps there is no reason why it should not be moved, indicating a failure in thinking in the first place.

An assistant who makes no decisions at an inspection will inevitably draw the amused or irritated contempt of a contractor when he is of an age or standard of training where he ought at least to know some of the answers. Where the assistant feels unable to suggest possible alternatives, the contractor may derive some satisfaction from listing some with their merits and demerits, to the assistant's gain in knowledge and goodwill, even if he still refuses to make a decision, which may be politically wise. He can only give his reasons: he is under orders. The answers to what may seem simple problems may affect the Building Regulations, fire protection, legal commitments or the client's specific requirements.

Among the awkward questions are those that inquire what certain drawings really mean. Perhaps the dimensions do not add up, or the small-scale dimensions do not agree with the joinery dimensions, or floor finishes on the drawings do not agree with those in the schedule. There is enormous scope for being wrong, especially when drawings are done in a hurry. The contractor should thoroughly examine all drawings as soon as they are received and then he should list his queries, including, as far is as practicable, the items on which he will need further information in the near future. He should also check specialists' drawings already approved by the architect for any changes affecting the other working drawings and because he lacks the wholehearted faith in the architect's capacity to check specialists' drawings. This, unfortunately, is based on experience. So the site inspection can also include a catechism on specialists' and other detail drawings, and the assistant ought to know the answers.

There is even now something oddly feudal about the building industry, although this is declining. The architect must follow the established etiquette on his visits. Failure to do this results in bad feeling, or exacerbates it if it already exists, with no benefit to the job. Where a clerk of works is appointed, he is the architect's representative and the client's servant. He has a position of responsibility without power, being now an inspector only as distinct from his previous status as having authority to act for the architect. Hence the architect and his representatives arriving on site should make the clerk of works the first contact. The clerk of works is part of the architect's organisation, so, for reasons of courtesy and common sense, he should be the first member of the site team to see the architect, and in private at that. The clerk of works will want to report confidentially to the architect even if it is only to say that the job is going well, the contractor excellent and the labour force adequate and competent. These are things a clerk of works does not say to a contractor in so many words, however else satisfaction may be indicated at that time. More often of course the clerk of works will have much more confidential things to say, such as pointing out that drawings are wrong, incorrect instructions have been issued, he is fed up, the contractor is not improving his standard of work, is claiming unjustly for loss of time, has damaged the facing work through carelessness and not through rain etc. These reports must be made before the inspection proper begins.

Having got these clear, the architect and the clerk of works should then call on the site agent with the customary polite greetings before diffidently remarking that all is not well, and could the site agent spare the time to come round with the architect? On large jobs the site agent rarely goes out of his office except at set times, and so he will ask if his deputy, engineer, section foreman or foreman can accompany the architect instead, although he would be very pleased to discuss the job on his return. Only when something is vitally at fault is he likely to be drawn out. This does not mean he is not aware of how the job is going, or of his organisation's shortcomings, errors and omissions. He probably goes round twice a day and discusses details with his staff at frequent intervals, but he probably does not have the precise knowledge of the fine points all over which his trained and practical staff have. The deputy is introduced and the trio sets off, probably led by the clerk of works who knows the least messy routes and how to get up to the various scaffold levels.

On a large contract there may be an engineer in charge of all dimensions, levelling, steelwork, steel reinforcement and concreting, aided by staff and a foreman in charge of each section or floor, so the trio is joined by the engineer and each foreman in turn. If the contractor leads the way it may be because he is not keen on the architect seeing something or other, such as collapse of an excavation which is going to set back the job a day or so, or the steel reinforcement that is getting splashed with mud.

The architect should really speak to the deputy who brings the engineer into the discussion and any questions the architect may put are passed back to the foreman and there the chain halts, in principle. Such a cast-iron procedure would of course be ridiculous, but the object is to preserve the authority of each level of the organisation.

If the architect is annoyed at bad work in an area he is annoyed with the contractor, *i.e.* site agent or deputy, who can then berate the engineer who in turn berates the foreman. The architect does not berate the foreman. If the architect asks the foreman a question which according to strict etiquette he should not do, the foreman is likely to reply with a side-long glance at the engineer and deputy, for he may not know what lies behind the question. Certainly no criticism should be voiced directly to members of the labour force. This does not mean the architect should appear to be remote, for this could be interpreted as being supercilious and unduly superior. In fact, the more inquisitive interest an architect takes in down-to-earth work on site which does not waste time, the more he learns and the better his relations with the whole site staff, yet he must preserve a decent professional restraint on his enthusiasm.

Where operations that are unusual in some way are in progress any points the architect may have as questions or as comments are best addressed to the clerk of works and maybe the contractor or deputy, for the clerk of works must be seen by the contractor to have the confidence and backing of the architect, even if the facts are less favourable. A clerk of works whose status is denigrated by the architect or his representative in the eyes of the contractor and his site staff is bound to be ineffective.

Although the clerk of works is at present reduced to an inspector, the old habit continues of issuing clerk of works' site orders. Strictly these could be ignored, but in practice the contractor accepts them in the knowledge that (*a*) they have been agreed beforehand and (*b*) the architect will confirm them. A difficulty certainly arises when the architect disagrees with the clerk of works and the contractor in good faith has obeyed the order. A clerk of works who does not know his architect well will have discussed the proposed order with him before issuing it. The distribution of clerk of works' site orders can be top sheet to contractor and first carbon copy to architect, leaving one copy in the book, for the architect has to confirm the orders of the clerk of works in his instruction orders as repetitions, not simply by subject, number and date.

A clerk of works on a large contract has quite a lot to look after. He ought to be on site more than he is in his office, yet he ought to keep records of the progress of the work, check daywork sheets, familiarise himself with fresh drawings, discuss the contractor's programme frequently, liaise with the architect's office, see the local authority officers, services engineers, specialists, suppliers and traders. His function is not only to inspect the work, but to facilitate it too, by forward planning which he must discuss with the contractor and at length with the architect's office and others involved in the contract. His interests are in fact so wide that the frequency of visits by the architect can be much reduced, and in large, complex jobs it is only possible for the architect to function by having a percipient clerk of works. The clerk of works' background is 95 per cent practical, the rest theoretical, for his reading and attendance at technical lectures can be as consistent as that of the contractor and architect. To what extent an architect's assistant should defer to or overrule a clerk of works is very much a moot point, both assistants and clerks of works being of variable quality. An architect or assistant should certainly not overrule a clerk of works in the presence of the contractor or his staff.

Among the duties of the clerk of works is keeping a tab on labour force and mechanical plant. An architect should also note these at his visits, unless he can persuade the contractor to send weekly returns to him. The figures are useful in building up a picture of the intensity of effort, but the picture could be false for the figures do not guarantee that the strength is being used to best effect—a condemnation of the contractor's organisation which the clerk of works or resident architect would appreciate. Figures of labour and plant are only useful if they are being fully employed, and a weekly report does not tell this. At the next inspection the architect can expect to see a positive rate of progress relative to the site force: if it disappoints him he can look to the contractor for an explanation.

Daywork sheets are a trying accompaniment to contract management for, in the absence of a clerk of works, there is little proof that all the labour booked was strictly necessary. The sheets have to be submitted to the architect, fully priced, within a week after the work has been done, so if the architect visits fortnightly the daywork could have been finished for 11 working days. As work should have continued, all evidence is covered up and recollections have become hazy. Quantities of material and use of plant can be agreed fairly easily. If a quantity surveyor is operating he may adopt a more draconian attitude to daywork claims by virtue of the contract data he accumulates, and, moreover, may decide to measure the work and ignore the booked costs. Both the clerk of works and the architect sign daywork sheets only as evidence that the work has been done and not as accepting cost implications. Where no quantity surveyor operates, however, daywork costs should be agreed immediately after the sheets are received, for the architect must keep the client informed of additions and omissions as the quantity surveyor normally does. To defer costing daywork sheets to the end of the contract when all circumstances may be forgotten is to invite unpleasant surprises.

It is rare for a contract to run without departures from original intentions. Changes are virtually expected in foundation work and other works where circumstances coming to light require adjustment of the planned activities. Soft spots in ground, undisclosed make-up of site, diversion of services, addition of a window, omission of a doorway—such changes require to be noted and measurements taken for the extent of the additional work which is not specifically daywork, but which can be charged at labour and material rates applied in the main bills. They have to be measured for adjustment in the final account, and there is no better time than when the variations are being made. They are not dayworks, though some contractors may record them on daywork sheets.

This is one of the points over which disagreement may arise. If, say, the made-up ground was not excavated to a good bottom at the same time as the rest of the stite, resulting in the excavating machine having to return from another site, the cost to the contractor in digging out the made-up ground would be much greater than had he done the extra digging with the rest of the site area. The architect at his inspection will ask the contractor why he did not take out the made-up ground when it was so easily identified, to which the contractor may reply that he had had no instructions to do so. The architect might then say the contractor could have reported this weak spot to him by telephone and thus received the architect's authority in good time, avoiding delay and travelling of the machine, even if it had required the architect to make a special visit. The contractor might riposte that he did not regard the made-up ground as weak, being in his opinion of hard material well consolidated and suitable for the loading, but the building inspector had condemned it at a routine visit a week after the site excavations had been finished.

Had the additional excavation been done as part of the site stripping and excavation it would have been measurable, but because it was increased at the inspector's request, from which there is virtually no appeal, it is a fair case for allowing the additional charges as daywork. This would apply as to moving the machine, but if the volume of material moved was large that alone could be measured at bill rates, but not if it was small. A clerk of works would record the position, extent and consolidated volume of the made-up ground, about which he would already have expressed his opinion, and issued a clerk of works order for this and for the removal to tip and work and material in filling in the greater excavation. The inspecting architect should do the same. There is no point in omitting references to hardcore and other fill and consolidation in the hope of saving money; the contractor will certainly claim just the same.

Every measurable variation should be measured and recorded for the purpose of the final account, but in addition it may be necessary to record them on the drawings. Clients are entitled on completion of the contract to copies of the drawings of the job 'as built'. It can be very important to the building and site users to have accurate drawings. An obvious case would be where a high-tension cable was re-routed to avoid a small additional building such as a security gatehouse. This responsibility is taken much too lightly in many offices. A clerk of works will usually (and ought to) put on record the change in route on an order complete with dimensioned sketch plan. An inspecting architect should do the same and not rely on his comment in a site visit report. This action applies to a multitude of small and large matters which adds to the work load but is essential to the effectiveness of professional work.

Ideally all drawings and subcontract and supplies nominations should be available to the contractor on his being awarded the contract. Occasionally this is achieved, but more often it is not and is sometimes grossly ignored. A contractor supplied with information only at the last moment, or after many pleas, cannot programme the work and is provided with good grounds for claims. There are times, of course, when the architect is unable to furnish information the contractor needs. There are times, too, when the architect knows that some alteration is contemplated by the client which affects, or may affect, work in progress.

The architect at his visits must bear in mind the contractor's forward planning and keep him posted as far as he can without breach of his client's confidential information as to changes in the offing, which can be very embarrassing. The architect may know that parts of the structure are being built which, if the client decides in a certain way, will have to be knocked down again. How far he can go to warn the contractor to go easy on that area is questionable; it may be the only area where he can at that time make progress, *i.e.* money. If he takes a hint he may have to release much-prized labour, while if he does not the much-prized labour may later be so annoyed at having their work knocked down that they walk off the site. Hints to the contractor may be desirable, but to the labour force never.

The architect, being aware of the client's thoughts long before the contractor, may include small matters like a proposal to bush-hammer columns at that moment shown as tile faced. As the former requires greater care in choice of aggregate and concrete placing, the contractor should be warned as soon as possible. If he assumes that the change will be made, who can blame him for claiming for the extra costs even though the architect and client decide in the end to accept tile facing? The contractor has been co-operative but he could have ignored the hint thereby frustrating the idea of bush-hammered finish had it been wanted.

The amount of advance information the architect can give the contractor may be very great, since many thoughts arise on site which would not be prompted in his office. They may be to do with fixings—whether ragbolts, drilled anchor bolts, plugs or dovetail slots may be better in some positions than others—whether a column should be widened in some positions in preference to making out later in timber or steel to meet a new common face, etc. As the architect's thoughts are some months in advance of the contractor's job planning, he ought to guide his thinking.

A contractor is at liberty to carry out a contract his own way so long as the ultimate building and site works finish as the architect intends. It was not always so: an architect could tell the builder what he had to do and when. If an architect wants some part of a building advanced to completion before another, the tender documents should say so otherwise he is on weak ground. Conversely if he wants part to be delayed because of some change contemplated he cannot order it without risking the contractor lodging a claim for increased costs and extra time and even being in breach of the contract, which requires the contractor to 'regularly and diligently proceed with the works'. There is inducement to the contractor to complete part of a contract early where this also suits the client. If it is of no advantage to the client he can refuse to accept that part before the scheduled date. On the other hand, if early handover of the part was not foreseen at tender stage, even if it suits the contractor he may not plan to do so without a bonus being payable which has to be negotiated.

As remarked above, the architect has no power to interfere in site works organisation. This applies even to work in progress which he thinks may not be acceptable when completed. He may believe that planking and strutting to an excavated face may collapse, but beyond expressing his doubts (in writing if he likes) he cannot require strengthening to be done. If there is a collapse the contractor must put things right at his sole cost and may be penalised for late completion resulting.

A most difficult situation arises where shuttering for concrete work deflects or bulges under the load of the wet mass of concrete and is often virtually impossible to correct. The architect's opinion of inadequate stiffness can have no effect against the contractor's opinion. A different situation could arise in alteration work where demolition is involved. The architect may be aware that as demolition proceeds loads and thrusts change which the contractor may not have realised. The architect cannot order the demolition to be stopped, but he would be right in requiring the contractor by letter to take more precautions against collapse, perhaps supporting his case with diagrams.

Demolition work is a sphere of activity where the architect does not by choice get too closely involved unless exceptional circumstances arise. He would meet the demolition contractor on site to make sure his methods are not going to create a nuisance or be a danger—points which should have been clear in the specification. In addition, however, it is as well to make sure the contractor knows exactly the extent of the work. There was the case of the demolition contractor who razed a perfectly good church, which was up for sale, instead of the big house on the adjoining site.

Any hazards would be drawn to the contractor's notice, but this is by no means always possible, such as the collapse of baulk timbers over a deep well or pit nobody realised was there. There was also the case where the demolition contractor might have been warned that certain vaults under a London street, being arched away from the building line, would not support any street load once the front of the main building was demolished, an oversight which caused weeks of delay, re-routing of public services and much other incidental cost.

There are occasions when the site architect has to visit neighbours, who are complaining about dust, noise and vibration, and try to mollify them on behalf of the client, while knowing there is nothing he can do to alleviate their discomforts. He may have an embarrassing time trying to get them to defer applications for injunctions while hoping that the worst of their causes can be finished before their solicitors can get a hearing. Sometimes a cash offer soothes ruffled feelings, but it is questionable whether an architect should negotiate this rather than the client's solicitors or other representative. He may find that the client is not prepared to appoint another negotiator so what can the architect do but fill in, being the most knowledgeable person. Vibration may be the most serious complaint. Large lumps of masonry felled from a height can shake buildings for many yards around, upsetting laboratory balances and other fine equipment, ruining concentration, shaking valuable sculptures from their pedestals and porcelain from its shelves. In one relatively small job, art works in an adjoining gallery were insured against damage for £400 000 which was more than the value of the building contract. The site architect had to pay unusually close attention to demolition.

Another cause of dispute with adjoining owners is the effect on right of light and air caused by temporary screens and scaffolding. No doubt these owners were forewarned of the work to be done and had been satisfied then that their rights had not been disadvantageously affected by the new building, but not everybody remembers that temporarily during the course of the works their daylight can be very seriously reduced and dust may require windows to be kept closed. This is useful training in diplomacy for the architect, but he is likely to be accused of dishonesty in not telling them before the start how they would suffer temporarily. But then he might not have known, for the builder in order to safeguard the adjoining buildings, may put out a fan to catch materials which might drop and damage them.

Where buildings adjoin closely, especially where party wall awards are concerned, the architect at his site inspections may often have to inspect the adjoining buildings to look at reputed effects of the new building work in cracked walls, movement of cased stairs away from walls, broken glazing, jamming doors etc. This may be time-wasting because a thorough inspection should have been made before the contract started and another will be made after completion when all or any damage will be noted, but it helps good relations to respond to requests to call in. Sometimes immediate action is necessary, as when a large window is broken through the contract works accidentally.

When the adjoining owners have appointed a surveyor to protect their interests, it is proper to try to get the surveyor to attend at the same time, but this is not strictly necessary at interim inspections except when disagreement is likely on some serious matter. The contractor is not supposed to get involved with adjoining owners as he is not named in a party wall award or similar agreement, but when damage occurs he ought to be informed. In any case, the adjoining owners are probably not much concerned with the etiquette of the case and so complain to him first. It is then quite possible he has a different story to tell, *e.g.* that the window frame was so rotten that it broke when the window cleaner leaned his ladder against it.

Acceptance of methods may be interpreted as approval, so if the architect is unhappy about any activity he should express his view. This applies widely and not simply to the work but also to scaffolding, public safety, unauthorised entry and vehicular access to site. Factory Inspectors are entitled to enter on sites to see that proper safety precautions are taken. The contractor has allowed for these in his tender and therefore he has no excuse for evading them except where they interfere with a necessary operation. This could arise where a safety rail is taken out while materials are being hoisted on to the scaffold. The safety rail ought to be restored immediately this operation is finished. If the architect notices one missing, a toe-board absent, or a ladder not lashed, he should draw the contractor's attention to it.

Safety helmets are not at the moment obligatory wear on building sites, but many contractors issue them to staff and the architect will usually be offered one. If he refuses it he weakens the contractor's propaganda and if he is injured in consequence he will have weakened a claim for compensation.

Public safety considerations could affect enclosure of the site. Where building up to the back edge of a footpath, the contractor will have obtained a licence to erect a hoarding to allow some working space on the footway and that screen must be adequate to prevent a member of the public from being struck by a barrow, length of wood, brickbat etc., and the hoarding itself should not be capable of doing damage by having barbed wire or projections, nails and so on at dangerous levels. The contractor is responsible for public safety, but if the architect thinks he is failing in his duty, or perhaps his orders are being ignored, he should inform the contractor, probably confirming by letter, for it is possible that the client might be coupled with the builder in a claim for damages and if the case were to go against the client he might think the architect is partly to blame.

Protection against unauthorised entry could be regarded as wholly the contractor's responsibility were it not for the consequences of vandalism and theft. Brickwork slashed with paint, lavatories flooded, brasswork stolen, plate glass broken etc. all affect the job and the completion date, so the architect has a role to see that the protection described in the tender documents is provided and maintained. Experience may show that this is insufficient, and guard dogs and security staff can then be enlisted, possibly with costs shared between contractor and client.

An architect must be fair to a contractor and fair to a client. Fairness to a contractor may lose him a client because the client may hold that an architect's duty is to extract from the contractor as much money value as he can, regardless of fair play and conditions of contract. Hence at inspection the architect may be under pressure to get a contractor to make an alteration, use better materials or do other work by some subterfuge or other without payment. This cannot be condoned; even if a contractor has made an error requiring work to be re-executed, it is unfair to get him to incorporate in the new work an alteration required by the client, such as moving the position of a door. Strictly, the contractor should re-execute the incorrect work to the architect's satisfaction and only then cut out for and alter the position of the door, for which he would be paid. This is time and labour wasteful and should be short-circuited by telling the contractor where to put the doorway in the re-built work, promising him payment, if he complains, of something like half the cost which would otherwise have arisen. The contractor cannot be compelled to agree to this arrangement but would be singularly unco-operative not to.

A similar attitude applies to work done by nominated subcontractors. Strictly, once the contractor and subcontractor have signed a subcontract, the contractor is responsible for the quality of the subcontractor's work and materials used. The contractor may be in a difficulty in that materials may be selected by the architect for the subcontractor's use without reference to the contractor who may only be given a description or code number. An efficient contractor will not be satisfied with either; he will require samples as approved by the architect and may require the architect to confirm that the samples are acceptable to him. This is to avoid substitution firstly, but secondly it enables the contractor to satisfy himself that he is not being required to allow the use of a material or item which he believes will prove unsatisfactory and which the architect will ultimately condemn, for while that particular material or item could possibly be replaced by better goods, the contractor might have to break up his own work to facilitate replacement.

Subcontractors should have two censors, one being the contractor (who should satisfy himself first that their work is well done) and the other the architect. The contractor should not be allowed to evade this duty by claiming the subcontractor and his material were chosen and approved by the architect by nomination, and that they are therefore outside the contractor's control. The architect is responsible for the nomination and must stand by his decision, even if he has to acknowledge the error of his ways later.

Where 'artists, tradesmen or others engaged by the employer' work on site, the contractor can be in real trouble for neither he nor the architect has any control over them. A point not clear in the contract is who is responsible for insurance against injury of artists etc., and who insures their work and its effect on the contractor's insurance for the building being erected; but the clause could be taken to mean that the employer is responsible for these, in which case the contractor would be entitled to require evidence of this. Then there is protection, if any, to such works. If necessary it ought to be the satisfaction of the artist etc., but it should also keep the contractor happy, for he will be responsible if the artist's idea of protection proves too flimsy. The artist's idea of protection may also hamper the contractor's access to his own work sites.

The timing of employer's specialist workers is also a matter which the architect should discuss with the contractor, who will not relish having outsiders working on his site. He has no control in the contract over their deliveries, working times or labour. The architect should negotiate with the artists or others and the contractor how their work sites should be approached on foot and by vehicle, how materials be conveyed (preferably by the contractor), charged, stored, screened off, electric power use and water use, contractor's protection from dusty, noisy and vibratory activities and any special conditions examined when protection from frost, not necessary for other work, may be important. In all, the contractor has a lot of responsibility and worry, just as if the artists etc. were subcontractors over which he has no control and from which he gets no profit. A perverse uncooperative artist can make a contractor's life a misery, but he cannot prevent the artist from coming on to the site. The architect is inevitably involved and must fight the contractor's battle for him with the client in the hope the client will discipline the 'artists, tradesmen or other' otherwise the contract as a whole may suffer.

Protection of finished work is sadly neglected on many contracts. On one contract an impressive spiral stair was allowed to be used by the labour force without more than sawdust protection for some weeks, to the ruination of the high quality nosings and treads. The architect was weak in (a) allowing the nosings and treads to be fixed so soon, (b) not finding out what alternative vertical access could be provided temporarily and (c) not ordering the contractor to fit softwood treads and nosings and risers on insulation board; of these, (b) would have been the most desirable, so avoiding damage also to the strings which could never be remedied.

Protection must be watched continuously, but largely this is a measure of the quality of the contractor and his supervisory staff, including the foremen. No tradesman accepts damage to his work philosophically, so he becomes disheartened and slovenly when it happens repeatedly. Insistence on effective protection raises the morale on the job, but it is pointless to complain to the tradesman;

it is the contractor who must be brought into line. The architect is nevertheless in a weak position for, if he requires work to be re-done because it is bad or damaged, there is no guarantee that the re-executed work will be any better. The architect can require the work to be re-executed yet again, but if the work is still unsatisfactory nothing has been gained and time has been lost. It is possible that on examination the better course may be to sublet the work, for the contractor may be just as aware as the architect that substandard results are all he can get out of his own force.

Sub-letting to 'labour only' gangs is frowned on by many architects, but there is no doubt at all that this long-established practice has its good points; they are able to do excellent work speedily and take a real interest in following out the architect's intentions, the more so if they believe the architect knows the fine points of the trade. This course can only be forced on a contractor through the architect stressing that the work must be done and re-done as necessary until he is satisfied with it. This can have two results: (*a*) the contractor can claim the architect is unreasonable, or (*b*) the architect must nominate the sub-traders, whose rates etc. shall be satisfactory to the contractor. The first reaction results in stalemate, while the second puts the architect in the odd position of searching for a service he probably knows very little about.

The problem, handled gently, may disclose in discussion that the contractor knows of suitable tradesmen working on another site who could be freed to re-execute the work shortly, the contractor knowing that nothing is to be gained by putting off a decision on a matter which can cost him money and sully his reputation not only with this one architect but with those with whom the architect associates.

On small jobs the builder is often adequately represented by his foreman, who, the contract acknowledges, represents the builder legally. The quality of a foreman is extremely variable, and he can often be a 'chargehand' upgraded for the purpose, but it would be unfair to suggest that these men lack capacity, foresight and administrative ability sufficient for the job. Many a good foreman remains a foreman because he likes an outdoor job close to bricks and mortar and cannot bear the thought of sitting in an office doing paperwork all day. A foreman or chargehand is good until proved otherwise, and the architect should investigate him as soon as possible. The foreman, like a site agent, will make a close study of the drawings and specifications as soon as possible and, given the chance, will ask the same awkward questions, maybe with some diffidence, as one in the higher echelons of the industry. In discussing the job with him the architect is for practical purposes talking with the builder, and the foreman is just as entitled to an honorific as the architect. He might be addressed by his office as 'Foreman', but this is less desirable. Builders sometimes have to take a chance in appointing a foreman, if there is a limited supply, and he will watch his talents as keenly as, or more so than, the architect, for the foreman can lose him money.

If the foreman does not measure up to the architect's requirements, he can ask the builder to replace him, but this may only revive the builder's original problem of how to find a good foreman. The architect may then have to deal more directly with the builder. Instructions given by the architect to the foreman are in effect given to the builder, but fluency may not be among the foreman's gifts and his understanding of an architect's phraseology may be suspect, and so misunderstandings can arise over quite simple matters. The architect must then cover himself by confirming all his instructions direct with the builder.

Architects have a poorly controlled urge to specify new materials or goods. Where 'Agrement' certificates are available, it may be fair to repose some confidence in the maker's claims, but many are enthusiastically taken up on the manufacturer's representative's assurances that the materials or goods have been thoroughly proved in use over a considerable number of years on the Continent or in the USA, and so must be good. There was the case of the aluminium slates, some of which were damaged in delivery from the Continent and not replaced for six weeks, and then in exposure some lifted in a strong wind and others corroded. It was then found that replacements were no longer available, manufacture having ceased! Someone must be the guinea-pig, but ought it not to be on the architect's own property first? Similarly with new methods: uncritical acceptance can lead to a sad aftermath, as those with long memories of past fashions will remember.

The contractor is once more in an anomalous position. He is told by the architect to order certain new materials and apply them in accordance with an unfamiliar technique. Trustingly he does so, probably at some cost exceeding the bill rates. In due course there is a failure when the architect blames him for defective work or using defective materials. The contractor protests that he did as instructed by architect and makers, to which the architect replies that the failure is proof that he did not and that he should have used his practical knowledge to adapt the materials and fixing to suit site conditions, and must therefore replace the materials with suitable materials at his own cost. The contractor can either do so or record a dispute but perhaps, as with the aluminium slates, materials are no longer available so we have the situation that some of the work is satisfactory but the unsatisfactory work cannot be replaced to match it.

Contractors instructed to use materials, goods or methods they are not confident of should cover themselves against future claims by accepting the architect's instructions subject to the proviso that, while they will use these in accordance with good known practice and maker's recommendations, they will not accept responsibility for failure due to other causes. The architect may feel ruffled at such a reservation, but his own confidence in his choice should enable him to accept the contractor's terms. If there is failure then the client has to bear the cost which may lead to a charge of negligence in failing to investigate the process deeply enough.

Workshop inspections can be a waste of time. Where the architect has nominated subcontractors it is presumed that he made inquiries beforehand so knows their qualities. Where an unknown subcontractor has been appointed, the architect should have investigated them between tender and acceptance. Where the contractor is supplying made-up goods, a visit may be desirable if the quality of his work is not known in this context. The most necessary visit is to joinery works where methods of stacking timber for air-drying or conditioning after kilning must be seen, where temperature control and weather-tightness of the workshop can be seen. Also where finished and partly assembled work can be studied for accuracy in dimensions, mitres, tenons, mortices and quality of timber for internal and external fittings, for unpainted, painted and polished finishes.

A visit to a shop making standard goods is interesting but ineffective in influencing quality unless a 'special' is being made. The architect ought to know the standard of work of the suppliers of standard goods without visiting their works. Non-standard products may justify a visit immediately before or early after the work is started to make sure they are adhering to the standard which the architect has set them, presuming he knows how to set a standard. A visit can be helpful in all 'specials', if only to make sure the subcontractors really understand the drawings, see the setting-out rods and templates, check that the joints are to be made by approved tenon and not by dowels, and impressing on them that no departures from detail can be accepted without his previous consent on pain of refusal of acceptance. One joinery manufacturer blithely re-detailed an architect's drawing by narrowing a panel left open for glass, ignoring the bold note on the architect's detail that this glass was a standard size of tempered quality supplied by the bank, with the result that it would not have fitted the door.

Delivery dates for subcontractors' work have to be agreed with the contractors. The architect may have reasons for advancing the dates, but he cannot do this without the contractor's agreement, for acute questions of moisture content and protection may arise. Serious trouble can arise when subcontractors fail to abide by set dates, but it is even worse when the dates are met with defective goods which must be condemned, causing delay in completion. The client can claim against the contractor for damages for delay which the contractor can claim from the subcontractors. This process rarely satisfies client or contractor. If the architect had correctly assessed the qualities of the subcontractors and had made more frequent visits, condemnation might have been avoided, which the client may point out.

Approvals call for good technical knowledge of a vast variety of materials and manufactured goods, so wide that they find gaps in the architect's knowledge, requiring him to get other opinions, not excluding the contractor's. A contractor will usually hide away goods he does not want the architect misguidedly to approve, and if the architect does select something unsuitable the contractor is quite likely to produce by sleight of hand an article he prefers and expound its virtues, to which the architect ought at least to make a show of listening to or regret it later.

Standard joinery should only require cursory examination if made to British Standard, but some of the workmanship is in fact so bad that the architect should condemn it if he has reserved that power, having relied on British Standard. He can complain to the makers who will often change the worst offending items if notified in time. It might be said that the contractor should not have accepted delivery of poor goods, but they cannot all be examined in the delivery van and it could be expected that the architect knew the standard of goods normally supplied when accepting the tender. On the other hand the contractor may in fact be waiting jocosely for the architect to show his quality as an arbiter of joinery.

Slump tests of concrete are easily made but are not proof of strength. Grades of reinforcing steel are not readily identifiable. Ballast may look good but it may have deleterious chemicals in it. The architect feels more confident with timber where shakes, waney edges and excessive knots are known defects when prominent. Bricks can be broken to see if the core is sound, and, having previously broken a sample in his office, if they do not match he can complain to the makers who might agree, confessing that a burning went wrong, so they will replace them as soon as possible; perhaps he had noticed, incidentally, that they were also oversize. Manufacturers sometimes have to get rid of inferior stock in whatever market they can find.

Welfare arrangements should not be overlooked at the architect's inspections. The building industry is slowly recruiting better educated men, but is tardily improving in particular its sanitary facilities. A good specification requires a reasonable standard to be provided and kept in good hygienic condition, also a weathertight, draught-free messroom. The contractor is paid for these so the architect should see that they are satisfactory, although some contractors regard this as an intrusion.

Progress charts are sometimes illuminating, sometimes almost useless. The architect requiring a progress chart or programme to be prepared for his approval at the commencement of a job has to base his criticism more on what he thinks he knows than what he really knows, lacking training, but he may see advantages not apparent to the contractor in suggesting revisions to dates for commencing and finishing some trades. A straight line graph showing values from nil at commencement to contract total over the period of the contract is interesting and misleading in its early stages, but later indicates what effort has to be made to take up the early slack. Most progress charts allow too little for holiday absences in summer, slowing down progress at a time when spare labour is least available.

The chart should be brought up to date after every inspection and at every interim certificate and studied again before each inspection to note what stages the various trades should be at. This is true of a large and complex contract and of a small and involved contract, but it may be unnecessary where a small straightforward house contract is concerned. Nevertheless, some kind of visual tab on progress and cost should be used to remind the architect of what should be about to happen and to help him to keep his client informed.

Protection of finished work is important and much neglected, but damage can also result from hurried drying out of materials, such as the use of heaters. These can cause high humidity which is absorbed into joinery and cellular materials to their detriment. The problem is then to balance ventilation with the desirable heat level. It is better to use heat only to overcome frost and to rely on through draughts to suck out moisture, with both sides of doors exposed and all cupboards left open. Closing down heaters at night in frosty weather may result in condensation being deposited on all hard surfaces. Heaters are a mixed blessing but those which have an extract ventilation system are effective.

Displaced protection materials must be immediately re-fixed. Door jambs and heads should be boxed while conduit, pipework, ductwork and cabinets are being carried about, doors preferably having been taken off and hung on loose-pin butts, window ledges of hardwood fitted then removed to safety. The range of protective measures is great and damage occurs in the most unlikely circumstances; *e.g.* the painter who stood in a coloured enamelled bath in his tackety boots although the floor was covered with dust sheets. One rarely sees protection on the scale one would like and this is understandable for protection costs money, and only a very explicit specification and bills of quantities can make requirements abundantly clear to the tenderer, who then knows that, despite all precedent, the client is prepared to pay for it.

The amount of damage occurring in a contract is in fact not very great, and it generally pays the contractor to make good any damage to the level which he thinks the architect will let him get away with rather than protect wholesale. Box protection to door frames would usually only be found where these were of good hardwood.

A high quality contract requires the employment of a contractor accustomed to that kind of work, and allows for the protection and careful drying out and correction of incipient faults which would be ignored by a less knowledgeable, careful or conscientious contractor whose labour force is not accustomed to treating with respect the good work of other trades. This is an argument for selective tendering for it is the finished effect which will please or annoy the client.

It is often recommended that a check list should be used at site inspections. No check list can include every possible point an architect should look at; if it did it would be so long as to be un-usable. Good site inspection relies on observation, and no architect on completing his tour should conclude he has seen everything he ought to see. He may in discussing his impressions with the clerk of works think of something he really ought to have looked at. This situation is not necessarily avoided by a check list.

Every job differs and every contractor and subcontractor has some different approach or material or method in his work which a standard check list cannot foresee. The better course is for the architect to ruminate in his office on the decisions made since his previous inspection, letters written and drawings issued and then make up his own check list of unlikely items to be looked at. If he has required a greater depth of excavation to be made at some point he ought automatically to remember this in his tour round the site unless it is at a point he would not expect to visit again. Unfortunately one's intentions can be too easily diverted at the critical moment which is where a personal immediate check list has its value. He ought not to have to be reminded to look at brickwork for bond, plumb, level coursing and pointing, or shuttering or steel reinforcement. If he does not look at these and similar obvious constructional matters he is a poor inspector. To be useful a private check list should be written out prior to every visit and prompted in some matters by his report of his previous visit: it should never include the obvious.

Clients having acquired expensive sites sometimes demand that a contractor take possession and commence work before the architect has completed his drawings and even before approval to the works has been obtained from the local authority. The local authority cannot stop this, provided that town planning consent has been given, but it lays the architect and client open to the risk that some works will be done for which approval will not be available. The contractor does not take this risk for he puts it all on the client who is prepared to take this risk when he is either confident that his architect is technically competent or he can extract damages from the architect for his failure. The difficulties start with the building inspectors having no interest in the work and refusing to look at excavations or any other of the stages of work normally inspected. Where it is clear that the client is a bona-fide developer who wishes to satisfy all building controls, the architect may succeed in inviting inspection by the inspector so that, when in time approval is given to drawings and calculations, the inspector has no qualms about making inspections officially. If this early co-operation is lacking, the architect must be the more exact in his records of work done for production to the inspector when he is able to call on his belated inspections.

# CHAPTER 2

# *Preliminaries*

When site supervision is through the appointment of a site architect his duties may be largely those of a clerk of works, or alternatively he may be largely responsible for co-ordinating site progress information with the architect's head office administration, with a clerk of works also operating. In the former situation the reason for his appointment is likely to be the complexity of the job involving many specialists as subcontractors working on a simple frame and slab construction by the main contractor. His job is more interpreting specialists' drawings and co-ordinating their activities, which demands a detailed knowledge of materials, methods and time scale not easily acquired.

The contractor following his appointment will make his second visit to the site, having seen it prior to tendering, and will meet the architect, whether resident or visiting. This meeting is to ensure that all the conditions affecting the site were understood from the contract documents. Some may not be as expected: telephone cables and high tension wires may still cross the site which should have been removed weeks ago; a nearby stream may be in spate, overflowing its banks as an annual event not realised when the survey was made in late summer. Some easements for services may have to be respected which have to be traversed. The architect must then urge action by the Post Office and electricity board and find out from the riparian authority whether they have plans to clean out the bed of the stream. If not, the stormwater system may need to be re-designed.

The contractor and architect will also check the site boundaries with the drawings. If a right of access is still being exercised which should have been extinguished, the architect has to find out why not and, if not immediately possible, discuss with the contractor how the right could be continued without affecting his early programme.

Where there are shared roads and bridges, the condition of these at time of takeover of the site must be recorded and assessment made of the kind of traffic the holder of the right will use, which might be much more damaging than that of the contractor. This can be particularly important where bridges are concerned, collapse being expensive to remedy.

There may also be adjoining owners to see, following up notifications that works are about to commence, only strictly necessary where an award exists but a courtesy otherwise. There may be reasons why exceptional noise would be a serious nuisance at certain times but less so at others, which the architect could explain to the contractor in an adjoining owner's presence, for the adjoining owner to confirm, the point of this being that the owner then knows that the architect understands precisely his problem. Even when there is a clause about this in the contract, the contractor may decide to ignore it and the architect's instructions to desist from breaching the contract terms, preferring to wait for an application for an injunction by which time he hopes the noisy work will be finished.

The architect may also have arranged for representatives of public service authorities to attend for discussion on temporary and permanent supplies, with particular reference to times, to be confirmed when the progress chart is in draft.

When alteration works are to be done, the usual introductions to department managers are made and approximate programmes outlined on lines previously discussed with the architect, reiterating conditions affecting access, dust, noise, security, traffic, welfare arrangements, parking and storage. A liaison officer is often appointed by the client to deal with these matters and keep his colleagues posted, saving much time and helping by one person only being the arbiter. Protection to some parts of buildings may be specified, but this may not be clear from the drawings or description. Demolition and renewal works can be done in a slap-happy way to the detriment of prized features not appreciated by outsiders, such as happened in the breaking of much crown glass by roofers stripping for re-tiling.

The datum for levels can be identified and where in danger of being affected by the works, arrangements can be made for protection or transfer to a new agreed position. If an OS bench mark has been used, the contractor may say he will set up his own in a nearer position, but the architect need not take notice of this, though once the job starts it is as well to make sure the first structural level is correctly related to the bench mark.

Trees to be preserved must be identified and proposals for protection should be agreed with urgency stressed, for few things are as vulnerable as trees once earth-moving equipment appears on site. Where crops are growing, the owner may have intended to harvest them prior to possession, but this may have been delayed by poor weather. A decision must be reached on whether the crops are to be sacrificed or whether the grower is to be allowed time or is to be paid compensation; but the last only if the building owner agrees.

If trial holes have been left open—a dangerous practice—they can be looked at largely to see whether water shows, and arrangements can then be made for them to be filled in once the contractor has confirmed strata. The positions of trial bores would be shown on the site plan.

The positions for contractor's offices, clerk of works office, mess-rooms, lavatories and stores can then be agreed. Usually the contractor has good reasons for sites selected which, even if the architect disapproves, he should certainly listen to, for the planning of operations may be affected. Hoardings may be proposed when advertising rights may be claimed by the contractor which the client might prefer to retain or gain. Restriction of entry by unauthorised persons by day or night would be the subject of a specification clause and the details could be discussed, but in alterations and additions to buildings, the works site might be protected in association with the owner's protection arrangements; these should be explained and the responsibilities assessed. In these cases the contractor should be aware of the restrictions, and the meeting with the owner's representative should be largely confirmatory. They might include barring the most direct access route because of some industrial process carried out alongside which must not be disturbed. Again it is necessary to record the conditions of roads and possibly agree to a weight limitation.

The date for taking possession of a site is seldom the day on which work actually starts, though visits from prospective subcontractors and sub-traders may be made, followed in a day or so by sheds and a day or so later by gangs to erect them, the team being built up as labour comes free on other sites and a water connection is supplied.

The first formal site meeting may be held some time after taking possession to look at organisation rather than progress on site, the architect being expected to state the position as to all nominated suppliers and subcontractors, their drawings, his own drawings, and to introduce such assistants as may make inspections on his behalf. These site meetings are not for clients to attend, as their presence tends to inhibit free expression, but they sometimes appoint liaison officers who can scarcely be excluded. The architect and contractor then often have further talks in private.

Regular site meetings are usually at four-weekly intervals, but this spacing is often too long where much detail work is to be done, so these should be regarded as report and planning meetings, and the site inspections made on other days which also deal with detail contract and subcontract matters. Regular report meetings are useful to set times by which action must have been taken on decisions made at the previous meeting. And if not, why not? Site inspections in the morning followed by site meetings in the afternoon are often a successful arrangement, except that points are inevitably raised in the afternoon which demand inspections after the meeting.

It is customary for the architect to take the chair at site meetings and to prepare the minutes, but there are good arguments against this practice. The contractor is in charge of the site and all work on it so the purpose of the site meeting ought to be to look at the arrangements for the future, the appointment and co-ordination of subcontractors, suppliers and all specialists. Representatives of the firms concerned attend only if required by the contractor. The architect attending too can show by his not taking the chair that the contractor is in complete charge. The architect may himself be put on the spot by the contractor or specialists if he has failed to do his part. This can be embarrassing, but it is much better than the architect taking the chair and brushing aside awkward questions. Issue of the minutes as quickly as possible after a meeting is necessary to remind those named that they have action to take. The architect is, however, often better informed for the purpose of leading a meeting in his knowledge of the history and prospects in the job and the authority the profession still appears to carry. The more need then for the architect, whether chairing or not, to be scrupulously polite to others, holding in restraint his own temper and those of others when diametrically opposed opinions are expressed, but seeing that all views expressed are succinctly recorded.

Site meetings are loathed by representatives of subcontractors, suppliers and the like, because they often have to sit through discussions on matters unconnected with their own particular interest. This can be overcome in two ways: (*a*) by taking the items on the agenda which are relevant to their interests first, releasing them from further attendance when it is clear no one has further points to raise, or (*b*) by the contractor having his own subcontractors etc meetings a day or so prior to the report and planning meetings with the architect. While this could mean the architect would have no chance to cross-examine subcontractors, these can still be called to report meetings. Strictly, once the contractor has signed subcontracts the architect can cease communicating with them on matters concerning progress, but he has the moral responsibility of having appointed them.

The minutes of meetings should bear the job title, state the number of the meeting, the date and time, listing those present and their functions. Whoever is chairing the meeting prepares the agenda and includes 'any other business' which, in a badly prepared meeting, will occupy more time than all the other items together, because of lack of foresight in preparing the agenda which ought to be agreed with the other main party before the meeting. Each item can be given a number and this number kept unchanged at every meeting until its subject is closed, thereby indicating at a glance that its satisfaction is dragging on a long time. There must be no doubt in any future reference to a subject to which discussion the reference is made, so an item still under discussion at meeting 13 originally raised in meeting 3 at item 3 could be identified as para. 13/3/3. The clerk of works or site architect should report his view on progress, and any special matters causing his concern, and give an indication of percentage of completion, possibly in stages. The date and time of the following meeting are included, the minutes finishing with a list of those to whom copies are to be sent.

The contractor is required to set out the works and be responsible for the accuracy and to make good errors at his sole cost. The architect is not required to check the setting out, but contractors often expect him to, which could be held to be passing the buck. The architect need not acquiesce, but he should make sure no gross error has occurred, such as building too near the road or to another building or at the wrong level. Unless he does this he is surely failing to inspect conscientiously. Having gone so far where should he stop? If the building is set out out-of-square, it could mean building for several weeks before this was discovered, and if it were capable of correction, it would nevertheless involve considerable delay. The architect's decision on checking may be swayed by the quality of staff the contractor uses. An engineer BSc would be grieved if the architect mistrusted his setting out. Yet the architect would be right to ask the engineer if he had himself checked to which the engineer might well respond 'Certainly, but if you like we'll check it again'. So although the architect does not himself hold the tape, he can satisfy himself the dimensions are correct.

Internal dimensions are also important, not only on lowest floor level but upper levels too. A distressing situation could well arise where a 9 in/225 mm brick compartment wall is intended to rise through several storeys, but faulty setting out at one floor level results in the wall not coming over the one below, the concrete floor slabs then taking unexpected strains.

The small jobs ought to be checked by the architect, overall and in their parts, ensuring that no figures have been misunderstood as '6' and '9' can be, or an error in dimensioning may have been made. A common failing, probably mostly in houses, seems to be the formation of partitions out of square with the main walls. This is not easily observed until ceilings are fixed or floorings laid, probably through chalked lines becoming indistinct and made the more likely with metrication. Diagonal checks are the simplest, but the '3-4-5' or some variant takes very little longer though a third man is needed.

Checking floor levels is not so simple but is equally important, both as to horizontality and clear heights. A recent building in Portland Place is reputed to have all floor slabs falling from north to south 3 in/75 mm in its 100 ft/30 m frontage, and in an architect designed and supervised house a fall in the first floor of 1 in/25 mm was found. There must be thousands of cases and these can be serious, especially when working to minimum permitted heights where an error can result in a habitable room having less than the permitted space. Storey rods giving the exact required height can be used with some floor slabs but not so easily where shuttering is set up for the RC slab.

Checking lengths and heights with the builder's equipment requires first that the equipment be checked. Tapes often lack the first few inches or centimetres, or are grossly stretched, and dumpy levels can be in sore need of adjustment.

Setting out of road improvement lines must be confirmed by the highway authority and the agreed lines should be solidly fixed with markers in concrete, the architect sending to the highway engineer a copy of the agreed dimensions and another copy to the builder.

Levels of public pavements must also be agreed which may affect the levels of new floors, and so the architect must check, if only by asking the builder what check he has made, and compare level pegs with local datum point. Problems can arise where the back edge of an existing footpath is intended by the highway authority to be reduced when the paving is relaid at some future date to conform with standard falls. To which back edge should the builder work? Some architects consider the builder should conduct all these negotiations with the local authorities and in fact compel them to do so by neglecting to take action, doing the profession no credit thereby and getting themselves distrusted into the bargain, which is reflected in the tender prices of once-bitten builders. A sharp contractor can make these unbusinesslike architects' lives very unhappy, but the good ones are also likely to get the same treatment.

Causes of disagreement are numerous and those that cannot be solved must be recorded. Delays are fruitful causes, due maybe to the non-availability of plant at precisely the right time, or of materials, such as a breakdown in ready-mix concrete batching plant, or a shortage of carpenters in the area, or wet weather. How many of these are due to the contractor's neglect? A bulldozer ordered for a certain day may suffer a fault yet be the only machine suitable in an area of limited supply. If there are a number of ready-mix plants in the vicinity it may be argued that the breakdown of one should not prevent another source being used, ignoring the fact that these are already fully contracted for on other sites, although this would be less acceptable if the other plants were owned by the same company. Shortage of labour may not be so much of quantity as of quality, and an inquiry by the architect to the employment exchange may produce a misleading answer which the exchange could scarcely be expected to understand. Justification of delays needs inquiry, but rejection of a request for extension of time must be based on the architect's full knowledge of all circumstances. If the contractor fails to record his request as the circumstances compelling it arise, he deprives the architect of the chance to check them. Wet weather is a difficult one in that some areas are subject to more spasmodic rainstorms than others, but there are weather stations all over the country including many at day schools, so confirmation should not be difficult. A resident architect would, of course, be much better placed to assess reasonableness of a claim for delay than one visiting occasionally.

Disagreements, particularly on delays and which may involve the architect's own organisation, build up into significant totals which may lead to notification of a dispute and invoking the arbitration clauses. Details of the circumstances of each disagreement are then of great importance in the architect's interest as much as in the client's. Evidence recorded day to day may convince a contractor or a client that a claim is not strong enough to be pursued.

# CHAPTER 3

# Excavator and Drainlayer

The practice of skimming off all topsoil and heaping it for re-use clear of buildings and roads is economically sound, but the machinery is less discriminating than the manual labourer. Mixed topsoil and lower stratum results. Depth of topsoil varies over the country from about 1 in/25 mm to 18 in/450 mm, but 6 in/150 mm depth is usually assumed. A trial hole may be misleading in chancing to show uncharacteristic strata.

A grid of levels is necessary, and a contractor may not be satisfied with a grid prepared by the architect. He then takes his own grid giving a copy to the architect. As this new grid foreshadows a claim, the architect ought to check it, but his decision on this will depend on the degree of difference disclosed. The contractor may have made the grid simply to get quotations for the stripping.

The top soil may be covered with turf which could be useful for re-laying around the building covered by the specification on completion, but there could be economic reasons for abandoning the idea. If the turves must lie rolled during the spring and summer they will be useless by autumn. Much better then to instruct the contractor to sell the turf and buy new later although there is not always a market for turf.

In clay subsoil areas the question of sulphates arises. Some local authorities insist on sulphate-resisting cement being used in all sub-surface concrete. Some sandy subsoils are also contaminated with highly aggressive chemicals. A local authority requiring special cements to be used will normally draw attention to this when the application for approval under Building Regulations is first discussed, but if there has been no discussion the first the architect may know of it is at the Building Inspector's visit to pass the excavations. The architect cannot rely on the local authority to inform him so early, so

local inquiries should include this question. As mass concrete foundations are only a form of stabilised ground, the need for precautions
may be doubted.

In ballast areas, confidence in this excellent base may be shaken by
the discovery of swallowholes or similar cavities in the subsoil going
under other names. These occur naturally where chalk, ballast and
clay are in close relationship, due to chemical action gasifying the
chalk as rain percolates. Some local authorities suffer seriously
from these and will warn architects appointed to do their design
work, but possibly not those engaged on private design projects. The
holes can be large and usually have no surface or subsoil indication.
A lorry disappeared into one during the construction of an airfield
runway, and some have been reported as large as 40 ft/12 m in
diameter. Geological maps are unhelpful in not showing this
combination of subsoils in detail. As the formation is a continuous
process which is only ended by stopping the penetration of the rain,
the fact that excavation for foundations does not disclose swallowholes does not exclude a later collapse. This risk could be drawn to a
client's attention, but how to do so without causing panic is an open
question. The risk to contractor's labour is not negligible for swallowholes come quite close to the surface.

Where swallowholes are known to exist, the specification will have
required some exploratory work to be done by the builder but there
is no standard practice. Pointed rods can be driven into the subsoil
at intervals to 5 ft/1500 mm penetration but could well miss a hole.
Junctions of foundations for bearing walls and corners could be
key points for penetration tests. An 'electro-location' method is
claimed to have been discovered for use by the originators' surveyors
and claims reliable results down to about 45 ft/13·5 m depth. Seismic
tests can also be made by specialists.

In some rock areas a rock shelf can overlie a pocket which, if
overloaded, can fail. In mining areas for metals and coal, old ventilation shafts are often covered with timber baulks below about
10 ft/3 m of ground; this is perfectly safe from natural arching until
a superload is applied. On one site for a factory, the contractors, on
taking possession, investigated a rumour that it had been extensively
undermined. The National Coal Board said they had no records and
no reason to suppose there had been workings, but there lay a hint
in 'no records' so the original estate owners were approached whose
admirable record drawings showed drift and opencast mining at six

levels in the previous 150 years. This news came too late to stop wasted pad foundations when piling had to be substituted. Local rumour has its value.

The use of excavation machines has exchanged accuracy for economy in forming column pits. When hand-dug, the holes were usually not far wrong and the sides were planked and strutted. Now where lines of pad bases are required at fairly close centres the practice is to excavate a continuous trench averaging the depth and width of the bases, raking the sides and hand digging the exceptionally wide base. Wholesale excavation on this pattern can result in very loose bottoms which must be cleaned out by hand labour. The system also creates a larger area for catchment of rain which in saturating the subsoil makes it unsuitable for concreting. The contractor is required to do all pumping to keep excavations dry so the architect can look for well points and pumps. This method also makes blinding of the bottom throughout its length with concrete most desirable.

Discovery of springs is a well-known hazard. Sometimes they can be sealed with a dollop of concrete, but they frequently thereupon find a new outlet near by which is just as troublesome. More likely the spring will have to be led to a drain to join a ditch or be taken to the stormwater system, but if this is connected with the local combined sewer system it would be strongly resisted by the drainage authority. If this is not possible the architect may have to authorise sheet piling instead; one way or another he is likely to have to authorise an 'extra', for springs are not included in the usual building costs risked by the builder.

Excavations for foundations in loose ground face the probability that spoil will fall from the sides on to the bottoms. While the builder is not usually required to plank and strut to sides, it may be necessary to watch that no spoil has fallen and either reduced concrete thickness or got mixed up with the concrete. Pockets in the sides of the excavations are tell-tales, and the architect, being suspicious, may require the builder to break out the doubtful base and replace it with new concrete. If the broken concrete shows no evidence of mud in its constitution the architect must arrange to pay the builder for the additional work through the final account. An architect may favour one form of excavation and protection over another, but if the builder has a strong preference for a different one, he must be allowed his way unless the architect is aware of structural reasons for his own choice. In this situation the point should have been made clear in the specification; if not the builder may claim that adoption has upset his programme and he may claim a loss.

Excavations to receive concrete whether blinded or not with weak concrete must be dry at the time the structural concrete is placed. It is difficult to be sure the builder has followed good practice every time, but a pit with water standing about a foot deep when concrete is placed would have evidence that the water was displaced by the concrete because of the openness of the top surface and weakness when tested with a hammer, but a smaller amount of water might be absorbed into the concrete. In fact, one well-known maker of prefabricated concrete buildings has a gang of erectors who dig post holes, erect and stay the concrete posts, throw a bucket of water into the pit followed by a dry mix of concrete finished off with another bucket or two of water until the laitance just appears to fill the voids, the supposition being that the sand will be washed with the cement into all the interstices. In the particular case where this was seen, the building—a motor repair shop—has not shifted at all over several years, to the amazement of the architect onlooker. While wrong according to Code of Practice this episode points out the fact that concrete so used is a stabilised ground, there being neither bending nor uplift on the bases. The builder is, however, paid to abide by Codes of Practice.

Drain trenches should be straight between inspection chambers or manholes, but often an obstruction is encountered making a deviation necessary, either horizontally or vertically. The building inspector has to be informed if a foul drain is affected, and most will agree to a minor diversion, but others will insist on there being an additional manhole. What will not be accepted is a syphon where a drain dips under the obstruction, for this soon becomes blocked.

Excavations for roads, being shallower than for buildings, are more likely to have soft spots requiring greater depth of hardcore, but drainage of the subsoil is even more important, for frost-heave can break up the surface. This requires that the land on both sides of the roadway must be watched to see that it does not drain on to the road, or if it does that land drains are added lying below the formation level.

If roads and paths are to be taken over by the local authority after completion, all changes, however minor, should be agreed with the surveyor. Where concrete roads are provided, the builder will usually make these at an early stage in the contract, but where asphalt or bituminous carpet roads are specified the builder will usually stop at laying the hardcore, using this as his works road. This often leads to dispute, for the hardcore becomes so covered with mud as to be unsuitable as base for the carpet. So the hardcore ought to be dug up and be replaced at great cost to the builder. On examination with the surveyor it may be found that part only of the hardcore is so bad as to be condemned, but this situation should have been foreseen in the terms of the contract; if not the architect has to do his best for the client which such an omission could saddle with extra cost.

Many sumps, pits and caissons have to be formed which demand just as high a standard of workmanship and supervision as the basement of a building and which must remain level and plumb, which can only be ensured if the subsoil and compaction around are of equal strength. At these greater depths water penetration is more likely to be found, and the architect must then give instructions for coping, which could be well-point continuous pumping or ground freezing. The risk with the former is that a good deal of sediment may be pumped out too, resulting in formation of cavities nearby and subsidence which has in the past cost some thousands of pounds in compensation. A decision to pump might have to be changed if after a while sand was found to be coming out too.

Extensions to existing buildings usually show foundation depths to conform with Building Regulations as interpreted locally and may be considerably deeper than those of the existing building. In discussion the local authority may agree to the new foundations being at the same depth as the old, where strip foundations have been and are being used. If the extension has pier construction the case could be different, for as all ground compresses under load the original foundations will probably have sunk measurably. To put new foundations at the same depth to take the same loading is risky, for equal settlement could be expected. Either one should go to some arbitrary greater depth or increase the spread, but this depends very much on the loading and bearing stratum. That one rarely sees cracks in a bonded wall where an extension is added may be a tribute to the cantilever strength of the bricks bonded into the old fabric.

Field drainage systems when cut by new foundation and service trenches pour subground water into the new trenches. The cut drains should be given connections to a new run of stormwater drains on the high side of the building continued round the building to join up again with the old drains on the low side. Alternatively the new drain could be run to a ditch. What would not always be permitted would be to connect these land drains to the local authority system, especially where a combined system exists. Some action has to be taken on discovery of such drains to prevent a high water table developing against the building.

Drainage ware is available in great variety and many have problems in use which were not foreseen when they first came on the market. Unfortunately some of the problems only come to light after these methods have been in use for some time, like the experience with pitchfibre pipes that by laying in stony ground they became perforated, that all types of plastics pipes became deformed unless precautions were taken and that flexible joints in stoneware pipes sometimes became forced out of the collars. Not all builders know the problems and precautions, and the specification, being minimal, may fail to make the precautions clear. The site architect then has to know whether the builder's methods are correct, but the builder may know that what the local authority will pass differs from what the architect expects. Much of the trouble arises out of careless backfilling, so the quality of backfill must be inspected and, where granular fill is required, it should be seen to be compacted below the pipes. Most builders have on their strength one man who is the drain expert and takes a pride in his work, but the architect should find out whether he has kept up with the latest developments. The same man builds the manholes, and here again local practice may differ from principle in that, in some areas, the bricks used are not up to standard, so the architect may condemn what the local authority approve. Plastics and concrete manholes are alternatives to brick construction, the economics of these being difficult to fathom, particularly the former together with the problem of forming substantial bases and weighting them down in wet ground.

Falls for drains are today much less rigid than a few years ago when 1:40 for 4 in/100 mm soil drain was mandatory (unless you could prove you could not make a connection) but 1:75 for the same diameter is even advocated by some authorities. The elasticity in attitude to falls is not without restriction, for the fact remains that too steep a fall leads to trouble by blockage. Stormwater drainage also is allowed flatter falls than previously, the BRE noting that 6 in/150 mm drains at 1:120 have been quite satisfactory. The main threat to both foul and stormwater drains is from trees and shrub roots, both by displacing the pipes and by penetrating into the bores. The slightest leakage from a drain appears to be an invitation to a root, so special attention might be given to cutting away roots of trees which are likely to increase in diameter near drains.

Hardcore is often difficult to obtain, due to heavy local demand. The architect may be asked to look at a demolition site to approve material. The brick or stone may prove to be soft and friable yet, unless he approves some sample, the contract may either be delayed for weeks or a supply may have to be authorised from some remote town. In one area, recourse was made to steelworks slag. The sulphur content was high and the cost of breaking it out by blasting was over a £1 a yard cube/£1.30 a metre cube without delivery costs. Even then it was cheaper than importing material, but clearly the sulphur was a problem which had to be overcome hopefully by covering it after rolling with polyethylene sheet. Extra costs such as this are difficult to nail down. In tendering, the contractor would obtain quotations for hardcore which he thought he could use whether strictly to specification or not, gambling on his powers of persuasion. If the tender did not require the tenderers to list costs of materials including hardcore, the architect would have little evidence on which to approve the builder's claim for extra costs for long-haul or otherwise costly hardcore.

Hardcore specified to pass through a 4 in/100 mm ring is likely to be delivered in large lumps of brickwork which a labourer painfully and slowly breaks down to a size he hopes the architect will not object to, but this has a serious effect on the clause that it is to be laid in 9 in/225 mm layers. In fact this clause is very seldom enforced, but it must be where the loads coming on the slab over are heavy. Cavities in the hardcore must not on any account be allowed, nor must pieces of wood joist, plasterboard, plywood, tree stumps, window frames or any of those miscellaneous items one frequently finds in a delivery of hardcore. The builder knows perfectly well these are not allowed and a good builder will sort the material out, but others will defer action until they know how lenient or ignorant the architect is.

Another hardcore material necessarily used sometimes is quarry waste, either from ballast or stone quarries. The former is usually undersized and both may have much too much small material to give good drainage and to lock well and ought to be screened, but if it is quarry waste it is because it is faulty. Sometimes this is because it contains clay which cannot be allowed, but a thin coating on large ballast would not matter.

Hardcore must be rolled, and the weight of roller should be selected according to the loads to be placed on the slab. For a roadway, a heavier roller will be used than on a building having only a lightly weighted floor, but sometimes only an unnecessarily heavy roller can be obtained. Two faults can result which the architect should look for. One is that the heavy roller will crush the hardcore into too small particles, the other is that the hardcore will be so pressed into the subground as to force the latter up into the hardcore, destroying its drainage quality and inducing locking of the parts. In both cases the only course is to have more hardcore spread and a lighter roller used on it.

Specifications often require the hardcore to be blinded with ash, which is becoming a scarce commodity, but it can be replaced by clay-free ballast. But binding is not always necessary; it depends very much on the openness of the hardcore surface and whether a concrete slab is to follow.

Drain routes are often shown on drawings without regard to their practicability. The bottom of a trench for any service must be at such a depth that both (*a*) no pressure is exerted on the service and (*b*) the stability of the structure is not impaired. These aspects can be noticed more readily on site than in the office. While the solution is to some extent dependent on the nature of the subsoil, it is as well to try to keep the bottom of any trench at an angle not steeper than 45° to any loaded base such as a strip or stanchion foundation (Fig. 3.1). A trench cut 3 ft/1000 mm from a strip foundation

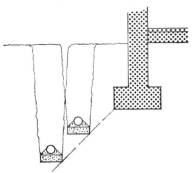

*Fig. 3.1. The foundation pressure line is shown at 45°, but this angle varies with subsoil and water content. Trenches in these positions could drain water from under the foundation and floor resulting in shrinkage of the supporting stratum.*

3 ft/1000 mm deep can be 6 ft/2000 mm deep in normal ground, but is follows that, as the drain gets deeper at its falls of perhaps 1:40, it ought to diverge from the line of the strip foundation. This cannot always be done, so the contractor must so strut the excavation as to prevent movement into the trench of the soil supporting the base and in addition surround and backfill to the service with weak concrete which will attain the same compressive strength as the subsoil excavated, which could be a mix of 1:12; this, however, need not be brought higher than to a point 45° to the foundation, all requiring precision in the architect's site instruction to the builder. Where the subsoil is stiff clay the angle of repose is much steeper than 45°, but if the clay is allowed to dry out it will crumble and let down the adjoining building (Fig. 3.2).

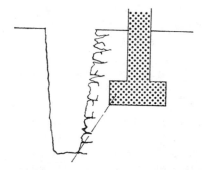

*Fig. 3.2   Excavation in firm clay holds up well as indicated on the left hand face, but even in damp weather it may dry out rapidly and crack, endangering the wall foundation, as indicated on the right hand face. Clay is difficult to consolidate so even if quickly excavated and backfilled an incipient weakness remains.*

Builders often lay drains about a building at an early stage so that scaffolding will not get in the way of late drain laying. If these drains are at levels below 45° to the foundations to follow, it is no good backfilling with spoil any more than it would be near an existing foundation.

Trenches for public services on sites are usually dug and backfilled by the labour of that service. The argument is that the service engineers are then satisfied that their special requirements will be complied with. It is exasperating when the builder has the capacity to do the work for them and his offers are rebuffed; and a programme can be upset because the service is not laid when intended. As the architect on the signing of the contract should have instructed the builder to place his orders with the public service authorities based on quotations and drawings already approved, the builder has no excuse for delaying placing orders except for the simple reason that he often has to pay out a considerable deposit for each for which he gets no interest. He may also have reason in not placing an order, such as for a new high-tension cable across the site which could be a menace to his building operations.

The water authority is one with a different attitude in that they dislike bringing their service more than a few inches on to a site, from which point the user must run the main. An exception to this may be where a meter is installed. A meter pit must be accessible to the meter reader, but not all authorities use subground meters, when a site has to be made for a wall-mounted or platform-mounted meter in lockable space not used by others. Such a meter obviously requires some length of main within the client's site and this is run by the authority and is stopped at the meter.

All public services have their preferred depths of cover to buried services which may be firmly fixed at time of laying. If subsequently there is a change of plan or layout, that depth of cover can be reduced which requires that the service be re-laid (or should).

An omission from good practice is the failure of the building industry—which includes architects—to provide permanent markers to show the positions of services. A stopvalve may indicate where water or gas entry is situated, and a small inspection pit may indicate a telephone connection, but the important electricity main has no visible marker at the boundary. It ought to be the practice for markers for all services to be set up and concreted in when the trenches are backfilled.

The planned routes for services are often changed on site for superficial as well as important reasons, and this includes drainage. The architect should record work 'as done' on his negatives, which the client will ultimately receive and which when accurate are invaluable to him when alterations become necessary.

# CHAPTER 4

# *Concretor*

Given good cement—not old, not 'hot' from the kiln—the quality of aggregate determines the strength of the concrete once the water/cement ratio has been fixed. Some concrete needs little strength if it is to be regarded as stabilised ground, like back-filling or void-filling material. This may be more suitable in fact if it lacks its usual proportion of 'fines' to create drainage passages. If a foundation pit has been dug too deep, it is usual to require the builder to increase the thickness of the concrete bed accordingly. This is salutary but unnecessary when 'stabilised ground' can be provided much more cheaply and be equally effective. Hardcore fill would not be accepted unless the loading was light or the feature supported could accept some small subsidence. Hardcore is normally required under concrete slabs but overdig may have to be corrected by filling with hardfill in rolled layers rather than in bulk depending on thickness or depth. The decision rests not only on principle but on perception and discrimination together with practical experience.

Not all areas have ballast or stone conforming with British Standards yet sound new buildings are erected. The compressive strength of the concrete must be lower than the Code of Practice requires so its cross sectional area has to be increased proportionately. There are cases where ballast has been condemned after buildings have been finished without modification of the structural design to compensate for poor quality, yet under load tests have shown no weakness. This experience lends weight to the suspicion that design presumes a fair amount of laxity in concrete control.

In some areas, too, graded aggregate is not available so one has to accept 'all-in' material. The problem for the architect is how to satisfy himself that this material is anything like correctly graded from fine to coarse. Sieving on site apart from being impracticable is time consuming so it is usual to estimate a fines/cement ratio which will give good strength with enough cement to coat the coarse material. The only proof of suitability of an assumed mix can come from a test cube which means at least a 28-day wait. Estimation of the amount of cement required must take account of the fact that a mix of, say, 1:3:6 does not equal 1:6 of all-in aggregate, for there is very rarely no increase in volume of the aggregate when three parts of $\frac{3}{8}$ in/9·5 mm material are added to six parts of $\frac{3}{4}$ in/19 mm material. It follows from this that a 1:6 mix gives a stronger mix than a 1:3:6, but this is scarcely worth bothering about in case the all-in material is deficient in some grade.

One of the problems of adjustment in ratio of cement to aggregate is that most sites doing their own mixing use machines taking a whole bag of cement, so the adjustment has to be made in the quantity of aggregate, which, if measuring boxes are used, calls for adjustment of the boxes.

Dirty ballast is another risk—clay, loam, chalk, chemical coatings or crystals—and difficult to clean. Washing is impracticable in large quantities and so must be condemned. Aggregate from the sea is contaminated with salt but this has little effect on concrete strength, apart possibly from delaying hardening and its propensity for sweating and unsuitability for rendering or plastering without removal of surface salts.

The first test of aggregate is the hand test—squeezing some into a ball. If it stays in a solid ball when pressure is released it probably has a good deal of clay or loam in it. If it cannot be made into a ball then it is too 'short' and should have added to it some cement or plasticiser (in the old days, lime).

Ill-constituted aggregate is difficult to recognise for, when dumped the 'fines' usually finish up on top of the coarse stuff, and so it needs to be stirred up to gain a true idea of the consistency. As in theory all grades of aggregates—$\frac{3}{16}$ in, $\frac{3}{8}$ in, $\frac{3}{4}$ in, $1\frac{1}{2}$ in (4·5, 9·5, 19, 38 mm)—have 50 per cent void, each grade can take two parts of the lower grade, so the question is which grade is missing in an 'all-in' delivery. The idea is then to take the grade below the largest specified in the aggregate and add some to the bulk; if there is negligible increase in volume this is the missing grade, if the increase is considerable, it must be a smaller grade which must be tried out in the same way. The proportion of void in the whole is found by filling the bulk with water, assuming the aggregate to be wet in the first place, from which point the experiments for void-filling can commence.

In approving concrete, the slump is the next important test and this varies quite a lot, but the architect seldom makes stipulations in his own specifications. The principle generally is to allow only as much water to be used as is necessary for thorough hydration and to enable the wet mix to be placed to fill all corners. A good batching machine measures the quantity of water added to each batch of aggregate and cement but this facility is not always available. When one relied on $\frac{3}{8}$ in/9·5 mm rods for tamping, or shovels for pushing the mix about, a dryish mix made for hard work and of course still does, but vibrators have taken their place very effectively. These can be over-used, however, so the architect must see that their use is stopped as soon as there is any sign of the mix separating. Poker vibrators must penetrate deeply into the concrete, but shutter vibrators obviously cannot affect the interior of a large beam so well and may bring the fine stuff on to the shuttering which is good for fairface concrete effect (if honeycombing does not develop), but it is bad for strength and key. Honeycombing is one of the difficulties faced in fairface work, for most attempts to avoid it are only partly successful.

Specified maximum slump sometimes has to be modified because the mix is too firm to flow around steel reinforcement, and poker vibrators cannot penetrate to help. If this problem arises the architect may have to authorise a much greater slump, hence increasing the water/cement ratio. This in turn must be compensated for by increasing the ratio of cement to aggregate. A mix originally to have been 1:2:4 may be increased to 1:1½:3, and test cubes of the latter should be at least equal to those of the original mix. All this information is set out in reference books but any mix can be ruined by bad handling.

Portland cement is very much taken for granted as to strength, but this is unwarrantable as strengths developed vary quite a lot, though they rarely fall below standard. Cement can be stale or fresh, the former being slow to harden and of reduced strength, and the latter being too strong in effect; but the worse feature is the quick set which its use can produce, though the 'hard' strength at 28 days will probably be satisfactory. A fast set prevents a mix being placed and vibrated, though this characteristic is not to be confused either with cements supplied specifically as 'quick-set' cements or with 'rapid-hardening' cements, and once a set has started further movement weakens the mix. The architect must see that the builder stores the cement in a dry place protected from damp air and used strictly in order of delivery. The risk is that new deliveries will always be placed in front of the first delivery which then becomes stale. Hot cement is really hot and can burn the hand, while stale cement may be lumpy but if only exposed to air may look as good as fresh cement. Bagged cement is easier to test than bulk delivery, the temperature of the bag giving the clue, but bulk delivery requires a thermometer to be immersed in the cement.

As the true strength of concrete is derived from the water/cement ratio, interesting problems arise. Use of chutes calls for a fluid mix having a good deal of water. Pumped concrete requires the same quality. Height of discharge can then be critical, for separation of fines from coarse is very important in all mixes. When RC columns are being cast in shuttering a full storey height, separation is a probability at the base of the column, but by depositing in small quantities and using external vibration this can be kept within bounds. Use of pumped concrete might overcome this but only if the hose can be threaded between the reinforcement bars. The same problem arises with deep beams. Continuity in deposition is of course also important, and the builder should have arranged that all columns and beams shall be cast in one operation. If small lifts are made to prevent separation and the concrete is to be exposed fairface, the lifts must all weld together to prevent joint lines appearing. This calls for organisation and understanding on the part of the operatives. Where beams are so long and deep that they cannot be cast in one working day, or for some reason they must be stopped, an appreciation of the design (structural) principles is needed, for the builder might plan to stop on the centre of a column overlooking the fact that in continuous beams that is the point where bending is greatest.

There are points about shuttering that should be watched, for this is a very neglected craft. Where exposed concrete beams and columns are used, the shuttering and strutting really ought to be designed by engineers (Fig. 4.1). Instead the job is usually done by instinct by an intelligent carpenter. In beams the soffits can usually be well propped without any calculations to help, but the sides are the real weakness. Ties through the shuttering can preserve the correct spacing but if one side has a lateral weakness, it automatically pulls the other with it, but of course only after the concrete is placed which is too late for remedial action to be taken.

Rain is a problem at all times on site but rain in shuttering is a

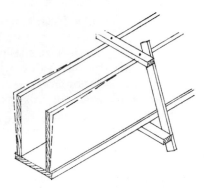

*Fig. 4.1. Beam shuttering as sketched is typical of what a builder may provide, although it is unlikely to maintain the correct section when concrete is poured, even if frequent cross-ties are added. Additional bracing or other restraint against outward movement of the top edges of the sides is needed. (Bottom supports not shown.)*

particularly mixed blessing. Rain helps to prevent the woodwork from shrinking which would let the liquor of the mix leak out, but when the shuttering becomes watertight the rain cannot leak out and this can saturate the concrete. Then rain might fall once more after the concrete has been placed and saturate the top surface. It follows that after heavy rain drain holes should be cut in the shuttering and the top surface covered over until the set has taken place, after which any rain will only do good.

Columns with wood shuttering are particularly prone to movement due to expansion of the wood after rain, and they may bulge, lean or twist and a lot of binders and stays are needed to prevent movement. This is all right in theory, but how the builder can fix a raking stay to each corner off the reinforced concrete slab is a problem he might with some irritation ask the architect to solve. No builder wants to risk having to break down an RC column because the shuttering has moved.

In concrete slab construction, shuttering must again be generously propped to ensure that no excessive deflection occurs; this is particularly important when working to minimum ceiling heights. There must be some deflection once the shuttering is removed, which will increase when plaster and floor screed and finish are added, and this may reduce the clear height below the limit.

Deflection being virtually unavoidable in simply supported beams and slabs, it happens also with many precast concrete unit floors. As few people bother to read the fixing instructions, the recommended centres for props are frequently not followed, leading to excessive deflection once the mass concrete infill or structural topping is added. On the other hand there are those prestressed concrete units which have upward curvature. Fixers can go badly astray with these, for the 'hogging' may vary from beam to beam in one delivery so the architect must see that the units are sorted so that those with the least hump are placed next to beams and those with the most in the centres of the spans, the remainder filling in according to the amount of hump so the finished slab has a concave soffit. If this is not done, the random placing of the units causes a lot of plastering troubles, quite apart from those arising out of the spring in the slabs. Spacing of the units is also a point to watch where there are precast infill blocks resting on sloping shoulders, for the greater spacing between the units the lower the infill blocks come below the soffits of the units. Incidentally there is one persistent point of neglect in the layout drawings of these specialists which may be encountered: this is omission of adequate provision for services to penetrate. In curtain-walling jobs, the rainwater pipes, for example, are usually taken down beside a column and past a beam spanning from front to back. If not watched the layout draughtsman will put a precast and maybe prestressed unit against the beam, preventing the RWP or other service from penetrating at this point. There is no need for this, and it should only happen when the architect has omitted to show where all the pipework is to run. As combined services drawings only come out of efficient offices, the architect on site may have to check the floor layout with a bundle of heating, electrical, pneumatic tube and rainwater drawings to help him; or of course he can remind the builder that he and not the architect must do this.

Concrete to be bush-hammered must use aggregate of a consistent grade and colour, and these can only be assured from quarries and pits which can guarantee to satisfy the requirements for the duration of the contract. This may require the architect to approve the quarry to find out what variations have been found in the past, what crushing methods are used, and what screening system is adopted, though he would not have much success in river bed extraction. A trial panel is necessary which is large enough to try out various tools, and an operator must be found who is prepared to carry out an extremely arduous job to a consistent pattern—or perhaps not a consistent pattern but rather a pattern which is contrived by varying the treatment. Whatever specimen is decided on, the architect must not change his mind except to coarsen the texture. This work cannot be done over a large area with small concrete mixing plant because continuous 'pours' are necessary to avoid batch lines appearing.

Curing of concrete has become much easier since the use of plastics spray has been accepted, but this cannot be used in all cases, nor for that matter is curing required to be assisted at all times of the year. Mild, moist weather is ideal for curing while hot sun with a strong wind gives the worst conditions. Tarpaulins can be draped tent-fashion over a slab to keep off the sun, but these tend to concentrate the strong wind across the wet surface of the concrete, defeating the object of the tarpaulins. In cold weather the same wind passing under tarpaulins keeping off frost can cause more icy conditions. Sun bleaches concrete and mortar, and an overwet mixture also results in a light colour, so the visiting architect might have difficulty in deciding which of these is the cause, and only impact tests on the concrete can decide.

As concrete mixes are now specified more by ultimate strength than by proportion, the acceptability of a concrete slab, column or beam is often not known for 28 days. As this is much too long, a 7 day test is also necessary. Taking cubes is usually the task of the clerk of works, as no one trusts the builder to be impartial, so the visiting architect should see the boxes being filled, dated and numbered, so that that part of the structure may be identified if the concrete should prove deficient. Testing laboratories can be universities, technical colleges and independent laboratories, so the boxes usually do not have to travel far. This can be important for they should neither be kept warm nor be allowed to freeze. On one job there was a series of bad results to the amazement of the contractors and the grief of the architects which turned out to be due to a fault in the university's equipment. This cost the contractors both money and time for work unnecessarily destroyed.

Breaking out deficient concrete has to be planned both to see that it does not extend into good material, but rather more to stop at a point of least weakness. Bonding of new concrete to old needs the usual preparatory work of a thorough washing off of dust and coating it with cement grout which should not be allowed to harden prior to the new pour.

Fixings to concrete designed in the architect's office may not be practicable on site, so early talks on this with the builder are desirable.

It is possible that more than one type may be necessary, and provided the builder is not extravagant and the systems he proposes are generally acceptable, in that they are not costing more or will corrode or slip, the choice can surely be left to the builder if he knows exactly what materials are to be fixed to them. Softwood has been used in the past a great deal and it still has its value, but mechanical fixings seem more permanent. Even as distance pieces, softwood might well be avoided as only material effectively impregnated against both rot and infestation should be used. Fixing plugs and heat-dispersed foam plastics blocks of diverse makes add to choice, but in the embedding of all these there is often scant regard for concrete cover retained to the steel reinforcement. This may not matter in practice as to fire protection, though the theorists would say otherwise, so fixings should be positioned with regard to fire protection.

Concrete retarders and antifreeze additives should be seen to be used only as the makers recommend, and even then their performance may not match the claims made for them. Retarders have a trick of varying in their effectiveness and the builder may be blamed for this. One builder, warned not to cast a ground floor slab by the architect in a day of dropping temperatures, persisted, adding to the concrete mix twice the recommended quantity of antifreeze; the result was a useless mass of soft concrete, possibly due to the excessive quantity, but also possibly due to exceptionally low temperature the following night, coupled no doubt with near-frozen ballast, cement and water. Aggregate which is frozen either in the pit or on the job makes poor concrete, which is not avoided by using hot water. It may be improved by fitting a steam coil into the aggregate hopper, a measure so troublesome that the architect would have to persuade both client and builder with great conviction to have it adopted. The method carries its own risks of course in causing too rapid setting of the concrete.

Stripping of shuttering must leave the underside supports until last, but it is equally important to ensure that the concrete hardening is not subjected to shocks by operations near by, such as striking shuttering on an adjacent bay or allowing heavy plant to rumble near by. Shuttering being expensive, builders want to strike as soon as possible, but the fact that casting is being done in warm weather is not a good reason to believe that the core of a concrete beam is as hard as the outer layer.

As the real strength of reinforced concrete rests with the correct size and placing of the reinforcing steel, it is strange that this has not become a separate specialist trade. In civil engineering one rarely sees the slovenly assembly of reinforcement which so frequently is found on a building site. The faults one finds are that bars are accidentally bent a little and crudely straightened, get coated with mud and maybe oil, are rusty with that thin film that defeats adhesion of concrete and are badly sorted in the stack. In fixing one finds distance blocks omitted, wrong rods used, both as to diameter and steel quality, incorrect spacing, inadequate lapping, slack tying, and the entire framework out of plumb and level. For designers who have gone to great pains to show exact dimensions and bends, it is exasperating to see the poor job so often made of fixing. The drawings are often very difficult to read at first, but usage gives power of interpretation, so it is largely due to the poor quality of labour engaged that reinforcement leaves so much to be desired. For the inspecting architect, checking reinforcement is a very difficult job, and in fact one that he is unlikely to be able to spare the time to do thoroughly. There are often obvious errors such as reinforcement mat placed at the bottom of a cantilever slab and a lintel bedded upside down, the word *top* showing clearly on the soffit. Checking is a responsibility the architect can with much relief pass on to his structural consultant, but this is an escape not available where design and supply and fixing are the subject of a subcontract. At least in this he can call on the builder to assist him.

Staining of concrete beams, columns and so on is due to concrete cover being either too thin or the concrete being too weak. In serious cases, the only course is to render the concrete to increase the cover, but rusting often does not show for several months so it is important to check that distance blocks are used together with adequate ties.

# CHAPTER 5

# *Bricklayer and Mason*

Bricks differ in character very widely as to materials, cores and faces. Bricks made from brick-earth, while nominally made to standard sizes, are liable to differ very much both from correct size and from each other in the same batch. This is relative, in that engineering-type bricks should not vary much, but less dense or variable-core bricks may differ by quite a high percentage. In a batch of well-burned London Stocks some were $8\frac{1}{2}$ in/215 mm long, and one freak was over 10 in/250 mm, all from the one burning. It is not that control at the kilns is faulty but subtle differences in composition of the earth affect the burning of each brick. This can affect size, face, colour and quality of core, and consequently suitability as facing material and for load bearing. The fact that a brick has been approved by sample does not mean that the deliveries will match in all respects. Brickmakers go to a lot of trouble to try to produce bricks conforming to British Standard and tolerances, but sometimes a 'burning' is unaccountably different from prognostications. This may happen on a large job where bricks are to be supplied from one maker over a number of months or even years, which can cause chaos in the rate of progress because it is impossible to hurry up the next burning which the makers hope may turn out correct.

Bricks for facing work can be of the through-and-through type where the face material does not differ from the core, or the face may be smooth, as if extruded or wire-cut, or it may be applied to the core immediately before burning. There are bricks made of fine quality brick-earth of mild red colour used each year for very many buildings which stand up well to exposure for many years and then are liable to break down, the face falling off and the core gently breaking away in turn. There is no cure and no way of ensuring that this will not happen. All the architect can do is to find out where his

57

proposed selection has been used for the past twenty years in the same locality and see for himself. This may suggest that 'rubber' bricks are in mind, but they very rarely break down.

Some bricks have frogs—shallow or deep—some none, others have holes through them. Some facing bricks can be obtained in 'specials' for 45° or some other angle on plan, others are not available in this form and may have to be excluded from the choice, while others can be cut and rubbed to splay angle without exposing a core of different colour from the burnt face—a laborious process which can perhaps be avoided by a different design of angle to the building.

Differences in colour of batches of facing bricks make most disfiguring patches, or lifts in brickwork which may never be moderated by weathering, so if a particular colour is required, such as 'plum' which is currently popular, every delivery must be checked for colour and size with the sample brick before it is unloaded. This is primarily the builder's responsibility but he may not pay much attention if the architect does not impress it on him. It is equally the builder's responsibility to check that all bricks and blocks are of the correct size and type, so that an error in size is not discovered only when the bricklayer points out that he is having difficulty in keeping bond. Some architects pay no attention to bond, being unconscious of the offence poor bond causes to other architects who see the work and to the craftsman pride of a good bricklayer (Figs. 5.1–5.3). In facing work, perpends should be seen to rise vertically from ground to eaves or coping, in alternate or other courses as design requires and not to wander off the plumb. Facing bricks of markedly different lengths

*Fig. 5.1. The lower panel shows the correct matching bond at the ends, but this results in intrusive headers which ruin the rhythm of the bond. This can be avoided by using a Dutch bond at the ends. Bond ought however to be identical throughout the building at all quoins, ends and openings, so for consistency a solution for one part should be applicable for all parts.*

*Fig. 5.2. In the upper panel the change from half to quarter bond to suit the wall length is very disturbing. The lower panel shows Dutch bond at one end and normal half bond at the other—a solecism which is however less disturbing.*

*Fig. 5.3. In Flemish bond the intrusive headers (dotted) in the lower panel are obvious but are avoided in the upper panel by adoption of Dutch bond at one end. A good bricklayer may find better solutions.*

*Fig. 5.4. What promised to be an interesting panel is ruined because the bricklayer has not kept his perpends running vertically one above another.*

make this difficult to avoid, except where a good bricklayer is at work, for he should look down the face of the building as he lays his bricks to line up the perpends (Fig. 5.4).

Undersized bricks lead to trouble in facing work, particularly where piers are concerned. The draughtsman dimensions the piers as 18 in/457 mm length and windows say 4 ft $1\frac{1}{4}$ in/1250 mm wide in a series based on column or stanchion centres, which is therefore inflexible. The pier width is wrong to begin with: it should be $2(8\frac{5}{8}$ in/219 mm) + $\frac{3}{8}$ in/9·5 mm = $17\frac{5}{8}$ in/443 mm. If the bricks come in at $8\frac{1}{2}$ in/215 mm then in one course it is formed of $2(8\frac{1}{2}$ in/215 mm) + $\frac{3}{8}$ in/9·5 mm = $17\frac{3}{8}$ in/439·5 mm and in the next course probably $2(4\frac{1}{4}$ in/108 mm) + $8\frac{1}{2}$ in/215 mm + $2(\frac{3}{16}$ in/4·8 mm) = $17\frac{3}{8}$ in/439·5 mm but as $\frac{3}{16}$ in/4·8 mm joints are not practicable with many sands, the probability is that in the former course the perpends have to be made much wider than $\frac{3}{8}$ in/9·5 mm, in fact $\frac{3}{4}$ in/19 mm (Fig. 5.5). In coarse-textured brickwork having flush joints of much

*Fig. 5.5.   The piers have been dimensioned to nominal widths, the windows made to suit, less 'going-in'. The result is that the piers are one full perpend wider than they ought to be to follow up from the stretcher bond below. In the left hand pier this results in double-width perpends in alternate courses and slightly wider than normal perpends in the others. This blemish is partly avoided in the right hand pier by reverting to Dutch bond, but this is not acceptable to everyone.*

the same colour as the bricks this may not be unsightly, but in the precise brickwork favoured in some current work, the result would be a serious blemish. The bricklayer sets out his bond at low level, first on the concrete foundation then again on the damp-proof course, so he should know what problems he has to overcome at this early stage, supposing always that the sizes of the bricks do not change later on.

While on the subject of bond, metrication may create no new problems on some work, but in others the use of traditional sizes must cause a lot of difficulty, in laying as well as translating from Imperial to metric. There is no doubt that Imperial bricks can be made to conform to metric measure for strength but with considerable loss of aesthetic bond appearance. Metric bricks are of course the solution when the new bonds are accepted, but if Imperial or traditional sizes are to be used the architect caring for face bond may decide that this should take precedence over standard sizes of windows or doors. But the draughtsman should get his brick pier sizes right first.

Metric bricks obviously cannot be bonded with traditional bricks for matching effect, but various devices allow one to fit the other. The 300 mm brick which may well be the more popular among architects is less likely to be popular with the bricklayer, for the addition of 50 per cent to the weight of a 200 mm brick can be very tiring by the end of the day. The bond principles derived from tradition can only work in solid walls when using the 300 mm × 100 mm size, but a closer of 50 mm may need a bolster to cut it, depending on the brick and bricklayer. The recommendation of the Housing Development Directorate of the Department of the Environment to forget bond where bricks do not fit the module is practicable but deplorable in appearance, though the suggestion is based on the consideration that matching pointing with bricks may obscure poor bond. At least it is worth the effort to try to work out a good-looking bond.

Common bricks are used not only where facings are unnecessary but also where resistance to dampness, chemical attack and frost are necessary, and this raises problems. Some local authorities insist on bricks for manholes and sumps being of semi-engineering-type, others accept almost any kind of brick. But the architect is in a dilemma for he knows that some much-used common bricks are likely to break down in damp conditions and he would therefore wish to use semi-engineering-type with consequent considerably greater cost. For local authority housing, he is unlikely to be given thanks for this, yet he must expect blame if he chooses cheap bricks which break down in a few years. The same applies in fact to structural walls below ground where breakdown can be even more serious. Consideration can then be given alternatively to the use of an approved type of concrete block for sub-ground work.

Much common brickwork takes very little weight but much also takes more weight than facing work, as in two-storey houses where the inner skin may have to carry both floor and roof loads, in addition to point loads from beams and lintels. Very little attention is paid to loads from lintels, although beams are given more thought. It follows that in much work the common bricks must be stronger in load-bearing than the facings.

Mortar mix is generally specified to be 1:1:6 because this is a happy compromise which can be used all the year round, if there is not too much frost about in winter. It also has a fairly light colour and does not 'go off' too quickly. Mortar mixed from bags of Portland cement and lime on site can vary in its proportions to quite a large extent, so the use of 'masonry' cement ensures that proportions are maintained. The builder who wants to get on with the job will generally prefer to use a Portland cement/sand mix of 1:4, which was in general use before the War, though engineers always appear to have favoured 1:3 which for most purposes is unnecessarily hard. Bricklayers would prefer the 1:3 mix because this carries more water—is more 'fat'—but both mixes can be used much better when a plasticiser is added, which is often the best course if colour of mortar is not important.

In walls of 'calculated brickwork' the supervision must be much more stringent than in other work, for every brick must be given its proper mortar bed and have its back and head joint filled. This is not what one gets in most non-load-bearing brickwork; the back joints and perpends in the middle of the wall are not usually filled except at the top of a scaffold lift, when the joints are larried-up to make the wall look tidy. In brick partitions, daylight can usually be seen through most of the perpends as it can also often be seen through 11 in/ 279 mm cavity walls which are to be rendered externally. This is not right, but provided the bricks are given their proper mortar beds it is doubtful whether there is any serious loss of bearing strength or lateral stiffness. If the architect complains that the perpends are not filled he gets the answer that they are left open for key for plaster or render. The architect has to make up his mind early in the job whether to accept open perpends or open back joints, but he would not accept either where calculated brickwork is concerned. This also applies where point loads are to be received from lintels and beams.

One of the merits of the 1:1:6 mix is the amount of water it carries, to satisfy the suction of the bricks. Suction varies quite a lot and is much affected by the weather, hot sun making the bricks much more absorbent than cold weather.

Sandlime bricks and flint bricks are more consistent in size than most clay bricks, and some authorities allow the former to be used in manholes while another authority will not, but in any case semi-engineering-type would be used. The distinguishing mark of this kind from the common type brick is seldom sufficiently clear, generally being only a colour smear on the bed. Sandlime bricks tend to be more absorbent than clay bricks, but flint bricks less so, the effect being that sandlime bricks laid for a couple of days can often be lifted off the mortar beds with virtually no resistance even when the recommended mix of 1:1:6 is used. To overcome this, the bricks ought to be well wetted before laying, and sometimes one sees the hose being played on the stack, and in sunny weather a bricklayer may even have a bucket of water on the scaffold to dip the bricks into. If the bricks are well bedded they are well supported and so are well able to resist even loading. If this is so, does it really matter if brick adhesion to mortar is not good?

Mortar plasticity has to be related to the suction of the brick. Engineering bricks have low suction and cannot be laid in 1:1:6 mortar successfully because the lack of suction enables the bricks to slither about on the mortar bed. It is then not possible to lay a sequence of bricks tapping each along to tighten up the perpends, because a number of the bricks are influenced by the tapping action and those not handheld move out of place. If suction does not quickly hold a brick, then the vertical joints must only be larried and not buttered on the brick. Hence what looks very much like slovenly bricklaying is actually the only practical way of filling the joints after suction has held the bricks, which will be a matter of some minutes.

Mortar for bricklaying should cling to the trowel for ordinary work, but may be too 'fat' for bricks of low suction. Sharp sand needs more lime or plasticiser in it to give it this quality, and so the architect may have to agree on an adjustment of the mix if the local sand is sharp and angular and not composed of rounded particles, irrespective of size of particle. Some sands are too coarse—as many grits are—for $\frac{3}{8}$ in/9·5 mm joints, and it is necessary to find another source of sand, screen it to eliminate the large particles or thicken the joints. Some bricklaying sands are eminently suitable just because they are not quite clean, having a modicum of loam or clay in them which gives the 'fat' the bricklayer wants, but this is not a line of country to be pursued as once such a principle is admitted more lamentable practices might creep in, like knocking-up again a mortar mix which has commenced to set. This often occurs when a lunchbreak follows the deposit of a new batch of mortar on the scaffold, but it is less likely to be of consequence with a lime/cement mix than a straight cement mortar.

In some areas, sand free from deleterious matter is not available, but despite this it has been and is being used for substantial buildings without serious effect. A chemical test with hydrochloric acid will indicate the degree of contamination and, if this is small, it can be overcome either by increasing the proportion of cement or by washing; but washing all the sand for a small building like a single house is really a very tall order. A test panel can be made of the sand as delivered and another with washed sand and the comparative strengths can be assessed, but only after about a fortnight to allow the mortar with contaminated sand to harden. What further tests should be applied depends on subsequent operations contemplated. If colour washing were proposed, it might be found that the foreign matter in the mortar was dissolved by the coating, leading to staining, while it is remotely possible that it might affect plastering, assuming of course that the sand for plastering used in the test was free from deleterious chemicals.

Mortar droppings in cavity walls cannot be prevented, but they can be reduced by the use of battens. It often happens that the mortar collected on the battens gets tipped into the cavity as the batten is lifted for the next run of wall-ties. A good bricklayer scoops the bed mortar on the cavity side as he lays the brick, but his trowel is wider than the cavity so this is not an easy operation, although it can be done with a slicing motion. The architect should look for clean cavities and insist on and really create a fuss if he finds bits of brick in them. The practice of leaving bricks out below DPC level must be adhered to, and he should see that clearing out is done frequently and while the mortar is soft. It is difficult to clear cavities in a long wall with no external angles, and this requires bricks to be left out at frequent intervals, probably not exceeding every 6 feet/2 metres. Even so it is difficult for the architect to satisfy himself that the cavity at base is reasonably clear of droppings; it can never be completely cleared, which is the reason for leaving the concrete infill top 6 in/150 mm below the DPC, and an explanation why cavity work built up off beams and slabs is so often damp on the inside of the wall.

Wall ties must be checked to ensure that they are correctly spaced, including double-spacing, where 3 in/75 mm inner skins are specified, but attention must also be paid to ties at door and window openings where spacing at 18 in/450 mm only is meagre. Where bricks are

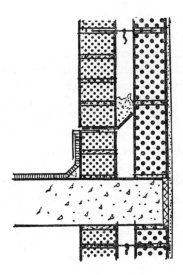

*Fig. 5.6. This commonly adopted construction invites trouble, the pocket below the cavity gutter enabling water passing the pressed metal gutter to collect, which is encouraged through failure to clear out the mortar droppings which are virtually inaccessible. A fully supported gutter bedded also into the inner skin would be much better. The thermal insulation applied to the inner edge of the concrete slab is unusual but desirable.*

used for the outer skin and blockwork for the inner one, differences of level often develop where the inner skin may have its bed joints lower than those of the outer skin. The wall ties that slope towards the inner skin take any water that may leak in directly to the inside of the wall, despite twists and ties.

Cavity gutters over lintels and beams are shown on drawings to rise inside the cavity about 3 in/75 mm and may be shown bedded into the horizontal joints of inner and outer skins (Fig. 5.6). By the time mortar droppings have accumulated from a number of courses above, 3 in/75 mm is obviously the minimum to rely on and is even more rash where the cavity gutter is of metal only turned up against the cavity face of the inner skin. Nearly all cavity gutters are made in manageable lengths and not continuous lengths so desirable where building off a slab or long beam. The consequence is that in some districts, where heavy driving rain penetrates poor external brickwork, even when protected by rendering, the water in the cavity has built up and leaked through the cavity gutters at the laps and over the top to the inside of the building. Unjointed lengths of cavity gutter should be insisted on, even if this means changing the specification or the use of self-adhesive gutter material which seals its laps, or a mastic DPC should be substituted. Some flexible materials used for these gutters can be pierced by brick scraps dropped into the cavity if they are not backed with solid material. If the design principle of sloping the gutter outwards to throw the water away from the inner skin is accepted, the weakness of this should be acknowledged and a cement and sand filler be formed in the cavity to support the DPC material.

Separation of inner and outer skins at openings by vertical DPC is accepted as necessary now, but at one time inner and outer skins were bonded, protection against damp being given by slate linings to the internal reveals. The objection to current practice is the resulting weakness of the wall. A heavy RC lintel, required to be hidden at its bearings, is then bearing only on the inner skin and its return to meet the outer skin, or maybe on about 3 in/75 mm of outer skin if brick tile facing is to be stuck on. Even if wall ties are specified every 9 in/225 mm in height adjacent to the reveal returns, the innate strength is low. Loadings from lintels are seldom worked out, as are loadings from beams, and slenderness ratios of walls at window reveals are seldom considered. This is irrational and must often lead to theoretical overloading of the inner skin. If the inner and outer skins were correctly bonded at the reveals, the construction would become much stronger. The only apparent way to overcome this would be to block-bond the two skins having flexible DPC snaking up the bonding. This, however, would still offend the pundits because the bond from the outer skin would in most cases be exposed on the room-side of the frame in the opening, and so theoretically liable to be affected by damp. A builder more concerned with good building than architecture may ask the architect to solve the bearing problem for him. The problem in the latter alternative is not only that of conveyed dampness, but also of lack of thermal insulation from the returned outer skin which can result in pronounced dampness on the reveals which is in fact condensation. A fairly simple solution to this is application of a thin skin of expanded plastics insulation material to the reveals—a solution which in most cases ought certainly to be adopted on the inside faces of the lintel.

Building in blocks of nominal 9 in/225 mm height may require the mortar to be not what is required for the brickwork, but something weaker, like 1:2:9. This may require two mixes to be used in the one cavity wall which will exasperate the builder very considerably. If the brickwork mix is used for the blocks it may result in cracking of individual blocks. These are usually lightweight concrete blocks which, because of the expected expansion and contraction, should have construction joints every 20 feet/6 metres or thereabouts in length, and compressive material where cutting up to rigid slabs. This is easily overlooked and does not matter in buildings having small rooms, but it must be catered for in uninterrupted long walls or the resultant cracking will cause alarm. Another facet of this is that in many cases fire insurance considerations demand that blocks of this lightweight character shall be used, but only a small number of the available makes of blocks are approved by the insurers, quite wrongly but mainly because the governing association has not been asked to approve a type of block instead of named makes. The architect must satisfy himself (and his client) that the blocks specified are approved by the insurers and then find out how to take care of the expansion gaps, which enable fire to spread from one compartment to another, to the satisfaction of the insurers. This is a problem that books on construction do not appear to cover and one that the makers of the blocks seem to be unaware of.

Blockwork is less stable during erection than brickwork and so cannot be raised in a large number of courses without risk of irregularity of face and bed. So blockwork often does not rise so quickly as the architect might expect, and the thinner the blocks the smaller the number of courses which can be built without risk of deformation of the partition. This would not be true of those little-used all-plaster blocks which should be jointed in gypsum mortar which hardens so much more quickly than Portland cement-based mortars. Some architects specify gypsum mortars for all blockwork because of the rapidity of building and absence of staining in the plaster. Tongued blocks are innately more stable when newly bedded than those with plain joints.

Plumbing of angles and reveals is sometimes treated very casually, and the architect on his inspections has to compare one external angle with another or rely on an in-built appreciation of verticality. One has to stand back and study the lines, taking care not to be diverted by other lines such as trees, lamp-posts and telegraph posts, and if one is suspicious get the builder to plumb some of the angles. This must be done early in the job or the resultant effect may be worse than accepting an outward or inward lean. At close quarters he can of course get the bricklayer (through the builder) to demonstrate the verticality of internal and external angles. The universal use of spirit plumbs is regrettable for small errors are easily ignored which would be quite patent if a 3 ft/1 m plumb-bob were used.

Level beds are also necessary and it need scarcely be added that one will often see humping of courses due to failure to check the height midway along a wall. A rod marked off in feet/courses should be handy to the bricklayers for use at angles and intermediately between, to be set on datum blocks at some fixed level such as first DPC, to ensure that all corners are rising equally. It is often assumed that because the angles are rising equally the courses end to end must also be but this is false logic; the sag of the line must be corrected and this can be overdone. Accuracy is of course particularly necessary at lintel and arch bearings.

Setting out of cross walls and partitions is generally assumed to be correct and not checked, which could have serious results if crosswall construction were used together with continuous floor slabs which prevent walls below from being lined with those above. This is evident, but less so is the need to check that the builder has set out all partitions square with other walls. A partition 10 feet/3 metres long only 1 in/25 mm off line makes for a badly fitting carpet. Occasional checks by diagonals or the 3-4-5 method are necessary and can be increased in number as errors are found.

Walls and partitions left raking for later completion are often built without using a line for the courses, because the other end of the wall or partition is not in existence at that time (Fig. 5.7). The result may well be that the courses rise as they run from the angle or quoin; this is not important perhaps in partitions which are to be plastered, but it is unsightly in facing brickwork.

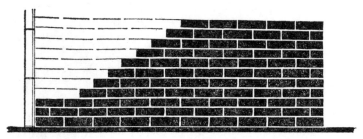

*Fig. 5.7. Brickwork beds may stray from the horizontal when the bricklayer's line is interrupted, a distinct 'hump' resulting when the raked courses are completed.*

Brick partitions—and sometimes block partitions too—are often badly built both as to coursing and as to verticality on the argument that, since they are going to be plastered anyway, so long as they stay up a good standard of work is unimportant. This results in the plasterer being expected by the architect to put right the bricklayer's faults (Fig. 5.8).

In extensions and alterations, bonding of new to existing brickwork nearly always leads to trouble in the bond where the existing wall is in 9 in/225 mm or 13½ in/338 mm solid work, as the existing quoins should have in one course one header with one closer adjoining it,

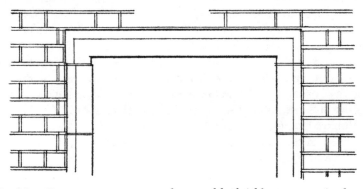

*Fig. 5.8. Concrete or stone surrounds erected by bricklayers are curiously more prone to error than when built by masons. The mason's joints of the lintel should have been the measure for the width between jambs. The brickwork bed joints are at fault at lintel level at the right: the bricklayer should have been required to re-build from eight courses down but this might have resulted in a more obvious blemish. Whether to regard a masonry jamb as a reveal or not is raised here where the left hand jamb arbitrarily breaks into the brick bond whereas the right hand one has orthodox bond brickwork stopped against it, resulting in poor bond above the lintel which does not happen at the left hand side.*

while the following course would have a stretcher. If the closer is left in place it looks out of place when the extension is built while the header is necessary for the bond on the return. The joint requires both header and closer to be cut out and one header only to be substituted, leaving a 2¼ in/57 mm gap for a new 9 in/225 mm brick to bond in the new work.

Pointing as a subsequent operation calls first for a sample panel— or several sample panels—for some finishes are unsuitable for certain bricks; a very rough-faced brick cannot be flush-pointed unless the architect wants a wide-looking joint smeared on the bricks. A hollow joint is much used where the mortar is smoothed and recessed with a piece of ½ in/12 mm rod, while some architects prefer a recessed joint with a sharp line at the brick above and below. Sometimes a sunk joint is suitable, sometimes a sunk weathered joint. The perpends are often treated differently from the bed joint. There are so many options that a lot of time can be spent in deciding, but this ought to be early in the work in case a sunk joint is chosen which can be made as the bricks are laid, avoiding the need to rake out all the joints subsequently.

Colour of pointing can also be important—a 1:3 cement and sand mix dulls the brick colour where a 1:1:6 mix gives a much lighter effect. The quality of sand can affect this also, coarse sand giving a warmer tone than fine sand.

There are parts of the UK where good bricklayers do not seem to exist, even the work which is exposed to view being poor. The argument used has been that bricklaying was never a local trade, masonry being traditional wall form, but after so many years this seems a poor excuse. The fact remains that masonry in the same areas is generally well done, both in traditional thicknesses of stone and the thinner facings now current.

Suction of the stone again determines quality of mortar in which hydraulic lime once acted as the cementing agent mixed with stone grit if good sand was not available. The nearest one gets to hydraulic lime now is probably masonry cement, but this may carry more water than the mason likes. In traditional work, the weight of each block of stone may be enough to prevent movement when an adjacent stone is bedded, but in the thinner stones the same problem arises, calling for a mortar with less water and better adhesion.

It was the practice when using Portland stone as ashlar facing to paint the backs to prevent staining by Portland cement grout. This staining can be seen on stone-faced concrete blocks and no one seems to worry about it.

In stonework supplied by a specialist, every block should be numbered, although if many conform to one size this is somewhat unnecessary. It is most necessary with random coursed stone, where the whole elevation of the wall is set out to ensure that through-bonders (apparent or real) take their proper places. This practice obviously cannot be followed where using random rubble facing so it is necessary to have a word with the mason to make sure that he knows what he is meant to be doing. Thick load-bearing walls are built from two sides and the core filled with scrap and grouted in, so the through bonders play an important part which cannot always be seen in the finished wall.

Stone fresh from the quarry when limestone type is relatively soft, and the face used to be protected with lime wash to keep it soft for the mason to rub down and eliminate minor deviations at joints. This is seldom done now, the power disc simplifying finishing off. This cannot be done where the edges of the stones are dressed and the bodies rough-picked, but the whole effect is so much more massive that such minor irregularities as occur are not likely to be blemishes. The dressed edges help the mason to keep to line whereas the rough-faced stones often used in random rubble are no help at all. Nevertheless the mason can plumb and line to a general face if he is a good tradesman, which the inspecting architect can check only by eye and an in-built sense of the vertical.

Thickness of bed-joint must vary with the character of stone, so in ashlar facing one may have $\frac{1}{8}$ in/3 mm or $\frac{3}{16}$ in/4·5 mm bed and perpend joints that are so thin that sand may have to be omitted and only hydraulic lime or its equivalent used, which takes a long time to harden.

Much stone facing relies more on the ties to the backing than to the mortar joints to keep it in place. Supervision of grouting the ties to anything like 50 per cent is virtually impossible for the visiting architect, yet laxity in fixing has many times resulted in facing being condemned as a danger to the public.

Some slab facings are tied back with metal and have mortar spots only to keep them in line on the face, so weatherproof joints are essential, thin joints requiring Roman cement or quick-setting Portland cement to prevent them being squeezed out, though match-sticks may be used as gauges and distance blocks. Fortunately this work is usually subcontracted to specialists who know what they are doing and take a responsible attitude to their work.

The only stone many jobs see is in copings where there is a conflict between making sure the rain does not pass the joints and ensuring fixed bedding. Stone coping bedding will not stick to a bituminous or neoprene DPC, but it will to slate or asphalt. Fortunately the sheer weight of each stone often serves to keep it in position, while rebated end joints ensure that even when the mortar jointing comes out (as it usually does) there is no direct path for the rain. The problem with slate copings is even greater; on one London school the slate copings on the boundary walls were all lifted off by the pupils, being at a convenient height for this purpose. The cure for this would probably be to use non-ferrous bolts, one per slate, through to the brickwork below.

Reconstructed stone is available in two forms. In one the whole block is formed of dust of the stone it is to simulate, and cemented with a toned Portland cement. In the other the facing only is compounded in this way and is cast on to a wet concrete mass so that it becomes monolithic. It is sometimes said that as two materials are used in the latter there must be differential expansion resulting in crazing, and crazing very commonly develops, and not only in this type of block. Some blocks are trowel-finished on the face which is quite unnatural and are improved with acid etching.

These products being compounded with Portland cement accept Portland cement mixes better than natural stones, but if imitation is required then the joint thicknesses must be those used traditionally.

Stones and reconstructed stones are all very easily damaged on their arrises which in ashlar work can be most unsightly. Fortunately adhesives are available which enable invisible repair to be done, albeit by specialists at considerable cost. Damage is so common in fact that stone dust is often sent with the stone delivery for the purpose of patching up damage which the builder may try to do using Portland cement with very poor results, assuming that the patches stick at all. This work really calls for the use of epoxy-resin cement, and the resultant patches must be rubbed smooth with a piece of similar stone.

Flashings to stone are traditionally of lead or asphalt, but there must often be the temptation to use aluminium, copper and zinc. Aluminium, however does not like lime, present in so many stones; copper stains the stone green; and zinc seems also to have its life shortened when up against stone.

# CHAPTER 6

# Steelworker, Smith and Founder, Ironmonger

One has to rely on steelwork fabricators to use the correct strength grade of steel as there is no way of identifying the qualities visually. There was the case of the lattice trusses supplied for a school and erected before the fabricators discovered that the tubes from which they were fabricated were of normal strength instead of high yield as specified by the structural consultants. Evidently the fabricators did not know from the way the steel worked nor did the consultants at their visits to the works, and in fact no one would have known had the makers not adequately described the grade of steel, presumably when rendering their account. The fabricators applied load tests to the trusses under the supervision of the consultants when it was found that the strength was adequate for the duty. This was fortunate for all concerned as no extra costs were involved, but it raised the question in the architect's mind as to why the trusses proved strong enough, for surely if the stresses were such as to require high-yield steel they should have failed?

There was also the case where a certain grade of high-yield steel was required for the suspension members picking up the floor edges of a tall core block but which failed to accept the essential welding of extension members, something no one apparently foresaw and was not realised until welding failure became evident.

The architect taking responsibility for all consultants' work could be held responsible and negligent and so should avoid having the onus placed on him. If, however, consultants are not employed and steelwork designs are invited from fabricators, the same sort of faults could occur and the architect could be unaware of them until there had been a collapse. A guarantee of compliance with British

Standards and Codes of Practice would help him to fight off a charge of negligence, but not necessarily absolve him.

Checking of both consultants' and fabricators' drawings would normally be an office task, but on site there could be also the check to see that the consultants' drawings have been followed. On one contract, cleats on stanchions to provide beam bearings were shown wider than the flanges, so that fillet welds could be run on the backs of the cleats. The architects objected to this on the grounds that it was clumsy, and required the cleats to be narrower than the flanges, the fillet welds being equally effective and the effect much neater. Nevertheless the cleats were attached as the original design because the workshop decided that it was the customary way.

The levels of concrete foundations, padstones, etc. can be checked, but there really is a limit to what a visiting architect can check so it might be sufficient to ask a few questions about these with the occasional level check where there could be doubt. This particularly applies where a solitary difference is called for, as at a lift base, which could be overlooked.

Steelwork when being unloaded should be stacked in an orderly manner, bending of members due to clumsy placing not being uncommon. Primed steelwork applied to grit-blasted steelwork can be badly scraped, and this must be made good before rusting sets in, *i.e.* immediately.

Erection from grillages upwards cannot really be inspected until stanchions are plumbed, bases grouted and connections of cross members tightened up, though if these are to be welded the temporary holding bolts may not hold the framing so rigidly as where all-bolted connections are required. In fabrication and in drawings too errors can occur which can generally be seen by comparisons with other members in a regularly framed building. There may be small errors such as holes for bolts not coinciding, requiring re-drilling for oversize bolts in coincident holes, but drifting of one of the holes for the clearance of the drifted hole on the bolt shank should be discouraged, as it prevents it from taking the proper bearing. In bad cases it may be necessary to reject the member.

The architect may be asked to sign a certificate of acceptance when the steelwork is fully erected, but this is the builder's responsibility when the work is under subcontract. The builder should therefore check the steelwork including plumbing of stanchions, but if he lacks adequate instruments the architect should satisfy himself in company with the builder using the primitive but infallible sheltered plumb-bob. Upper levels ought also to be checked by instrument but this seldom is done, although a visual check can still be made (Fig. 6.1).

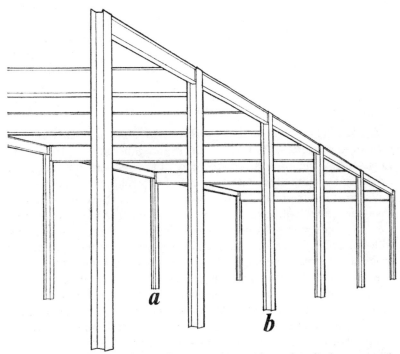

Fig. 6.1.  *Comparison of line of one stanchion with another discloses errors in verticality before instrument tests are applied, the architect then knowing that the steelwork plumbing has not been checked so his approval must be deferred. The stanchion at b is clearly out of plumb but so is that at a.*

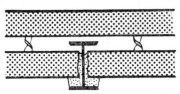

Fig. 6.2.  *Where stanchions are intended to take wind loading on walls, as buttressing, this arrangement enables the stanchion to receive positive wind pressure but it cannot take the negative pressure because the inner brickwork has not been pointed to the flange in the cavity—a position which the inspecting architect cannot see. A safer arrangement would be where the cavity side of the inner skin is in tight contact with the stanchion flange.*

Grouting of stanchion bases may leave air pockets even though airholes are provided, and excessively wet grout may be used. Taper washers may be omitted under bolt heads and nuts or be to the wrong taper. Bolts are frequently omitted while the adoption of turned bolts and friction-grip bolts adds to the matters requiring attention.

In the miscellany of other steel and cast iron supplies there are a multitude of items requiring inspection. Steel escape stairs added to buildings rely on accuracy of surveys which through small errors result in serious changes from the approved drawings with possible serious repercussions, such as reduced headroom, so that they do not conform with the Building Regulations, or otherwise offend approved standards.

Among the problems of steelwork protection is the availability of galvanising capacity. As this should follow fabrication it frequently causes delay but in addition there is often a severe limitation on length and height of the unit which calls for breaking down to smaller units. This in turn results in joints being only partly galvanised and thus requiring 'cold galvanising' to achieve even approximately similar protection; but this can easily be overlooked when painting follows. Pressed steelwork can easily be bent accidentally, and the cracked galvanising membrane is often made worse when straightened.

Metal windows although delivered crated often become damaged prior to fixing. When made of ungalvanised mild steel they can sometimes be straightened, but it is doubtful if the practice can be condoned where galvanised steel and aluminium alloy windows or doors are concerned. Fixing screws must also be protected against corrosion, and mastic bedding and pointing be continuous and of the correct quality, in colour, adhesion and stability.

Fixing of the miscellany calls for a variety of materials, some of which are not in the architect's vocabulary, such as the synthetic resin based materials. Cement and sand grouting remains the most common practice despite the very considerable shrinkage which may develop in drying out and the messy pointing which often results. Running railing newels in lead into plinths is still the superior method but is seldom really necessary, and caulking with lead wool is often better than any other method for newels and the stays of cat ladders, etc., but the inspection has to be made at the right time before pointing hides the inner work.

Fittings on metal windows, lantern lights, dome lights and similar items have to be checked against the specification, in particular as to location, for a window may open outwards unrestricted on an upper floor but be at head height to a passer-by on the ground floor, requiring some limiting device to be fitted. There may also be consideration of aspect in direction of opening, to be shielded against the prevailing wind or against the north wind which the drawings may fail to note. Some hoppers need long arms, others may need cords or opening gear, which the architect may have to sort out with the builder. He should also see that all protective tape is kept in place on aluminium alloy frames.

Fastenings on metal doors and gates are supplied by the makers, and the architect has to be sure that the locks are of a standard acceptable to the clients and the insurers and at the same time satisfy the escape requirements—these not infrequently being in conflict. Mastering of locks may produce the problem where the case fitted to a metal door is unsuitable for a movement coming under the master system. Gates can be made secure in many ways from inside, outside or both, so the client's intended use has to be explored. Makers of gates know a great deal more about structural design than architects, who may make elementary errors like the gates for a large sorting office which had the hinge pins out of line to make them self-closing but also required quadrant tracks and castors laid level on the roadway: the complaint that the gates were very difficult to close was understandable.

The ironmongery schedule on a large building requires hours of study with the client, but a house is even more personal and so must have the client's approval. Means of escape now figure strongly, following the Shops, Offices and Railway Premises Act, and require agreement with the fire authority on the locking methods of all escape doors and essentially non-locking precautions on draught doors, together with devices to keep these closed. This can cause much annoyance to the client when personnel, who frequently pass through, hook the doors open in breach of the fire protection requirements. The architect may be instructed to have the hooks fixed, but he cannot do this when he is well aware that a breach is thus caused.

Adoption of a master system for locks is important for some buildings, such as hotels, but it can be a nuisance in others, if only because a broken lock takes a long time to replace. Duplicate keys for every 'differ' may be much the better solution.

Fire protection also affects the material of the hinge, nylon being unsuitable on $\frac{1}{2}$ hour and 1 hour protective doors, and the architect must also verify that it has the correct number of hinges. Approval of samples submitted by the builder discloses a very wide range in design and quality of hinge, handle, lock, bolt and surface fittings, and a lot of time can be wasted if a tight specification has not been prepared by an architect who knows his ironmongery—a very deep and complicated subject.

The architect should see that every door is hung to stay open at any degree of opening; if it does not it is not hung with hinges plumb. All screws must be of matching material and fill the countersinks, except in the case of nylon hinges. Sometimes mortice locks are specified for $1\frac{3}{8}$ in/35 mm doors which are really too thin for these, with the result that the faces of the doors bulge. Semi-sunk or 'rim' patterns are much more suitable and cheaper to fix. Projection or 'throw' of a lock bolt varies very much and may not be important on internal doors unaffected by moisture content movement. The larger the lock the larger the movement in all probability, but some locks are 'double-throw' which means the bolt is moved farther by turning the key twice and so makes an external door more secure.

Doors or wooden gates affected by exposure to the weather should have their slide bolts of the barrel bolt variety fixed horizontally if possible to allow for movement in width, but if this is impossible a slot socket in floor or ground is better than a round socket. Bolts also are available in a wide variety, the sizes having little relationship to actual strength and strength of material into which the bolt shoots.

Aluminium alloy is much in use, although it may not offer the years of service of other metals, but the surface protection is also a consideration. Used externally it must be anodised, but many designs for external use do not stand up to the weather without surface deterioration within a few months, despite the claim that they are anodised. On internal fittings this may not be so important, but in time unanodised surfaces will become degraded unless deliberately cleaned, so the architect has to satisfy himself on these matters. Another metal on which he can be misled is BMA, which is interpreted generally as bronze metal alloy but may mean bronze metal antique, the latter being a surface treatment for brass to resemble bronze which in time wears off. In use the colour of the former may become brighter where touched by hand, but the basic lustre is characteristic. Matching screws are supplied but somehow brass screws are often used. On the other hand black iron strap hinges can be obtained but not black iron screws—only japanned screws which do not match, although black iron coach screws are available.

Wearing quality may not be self-evident. Some aluminium latches are supplied with stamped aluminium staples which wear out in two or three years in houses, although there is an alternative design in die-stamped zinc which is much longer lasting and matches fairly well. Lock bolts for industrial use must have good bearing area on the forends, so a good thickness of case metal is necessary or a good thickness of separate forends, and the fit must be such that there is little side play, on the lock bolt as on the spring latchbolt. To study the machining of followers and levers, all locks should be taken apart except cylinder types (which are not designed for the tumbler system to be interfered with) but this should be done carefully so that the springs do not fly out in all directions. Smoothness of action of the key on the levers in locking and unlocking indicates the quality of a lever lock, the number of 'levers' ranging generally from one, in the simplest lock, to two or three in those for general use, to five, which is the least number satisfying insurers, whether in a mortice lock or padlock. A five lever lock is, however, unnecessarily elaborate for use on a door which can be broken down without great effort. Cylinder or tumbler systems can be used as springbolt 'night latches' and 'deadbolt locks', usually being operable by key on one side and knob on the other, but some patterns have key operation for both sides. Often the requirement allows the use of either cylinder or lever locks, but sometimes one system may show marked advantages over the other. Cylinder systems allow of mastering in great range and can have mortice, semi-sunk and rim cases, but there can be problems in matching furniture with that for level action types. A further point about the cylinder system is that some patterns can be dead-locked and most can have the springbolt held recessed by a snib, features not found on latches in the 'lock' family. Objection can be made to springbolt night latches on the external doors of some dwellings, but, as always, a schedule has to be examined with the client to ensure proper choices are made.

Letter plates submitted are almost certainly to be made to the Post Office recommended sizes. The largest sizes of these permit a slim arm to pass so it is essential that such letter plates should not be fixed within 18 in/450 mm of the knob of the door's night latch. Fixing of letter plates to wood has for many years been by bolts having nuts turned on them on the insides of the doors—a most crude fixing which may still be offered, the preferred alternative being slot-screws driven from the inside face of the door, into the tapped holes on the backs of the plates. Fixing height is also subject to a Post Office recommendation, but another factor is privacy, the height being such that neither children nor adults can look through to the inside.

Spring closing devices include floor springs, heel springs, jamb springs, head springs and bracket springs. The first usually requires 2 in/50 mm thickness of floor screed, but some designs can be set in less, while bracket closers are those which are attached to cast iron brackets fixed to the door head of a door opening outwards at what is often now a dangerously low level, just over 6 ft/1900 mm from the floor when a 6 ft 6 in/2040 mm door is used. There are many patterns of spring closers for attachment to doors and door heads, and they are made in three strengths of spring. When a spring closer is to be fitted to an inward opening entrance door, only the strongest should be selected, to enable the closer to overcome wind force.

When required on inward opening doors hung near to a partition at right angles, the closer may strike the partitions before the doors reach 90° if fixed on the inner faces of the doors. When fitted to pairs of doors having rebated meeting edges, one 'selector' is needed for every pair to compel the leaves to close in the proper order.

Some escape doors must be kept locked by key for security reasons, and it is then necessary that the key for each shall be kept in a keybox with a glass front fixed next to the door, often made as a 'one-off' item by the carpenter but rather more elegantly available in plastics.

Mat rims are available to standard mat sizes and thicknesses, which may have to be varied to suit the pattern of floor tile, and as this often cannot be settled until the floor is laid considerable delay results when a cocofibre mat is required. Adaptable mat frames are available which can be fitted as soon as the flooring is laid, so protecting the edges. Unfortunately all mat rims are liable to distortion so must be inspected to see that when fixed they are square and undamaged. Floor separation strip between materials must be provided by the builder, but separation strip for bay separation as in terrazzo flooring is provided by the floor layers, which requires co-ordination in colour, thickness and material by the architect.

An omission from the ironmongery schedule is the entrance bell press, because this is an item the electrician supplies and it very often cannot be made to match in pattern or material the selected door furniture. It ought to be an ironmongery item because of this and the requirement, which frequently arises, for the house number to be incorporated. But being an electrician's item, this results—if one is not wary—in the bell press being fixed at the electrician's idea of a proper level and not the architect's, who may wish it to range with the cylinder nightlatch rose.

Door labels and numbers fixed by pins on the backs are often fixed off horizontal, and some doors with closers close with too much force, requiring the subsequent addition of rebate buffers, not all spring closers having check action. Kicking plates, desirable on self-closing doors, are not much use where trays and trolleys have to pass through; those sheared from sheet metal should have the corners rounded as they are often dangerously sharp. The suppliers should attend to this but will not unless the architect insists on it, at consequent increased cost.

# CHAPTER 7

# *Claddings*

This comprehensive term carries with it a multiplicity of problems and exposes chasms of ignorance in the architect and tradesmen. While the common aim is simply to keep wind and water out of the building, the different claddings have their own ways of admitting these. Tongued and grooved types fixed horizontally may shrink excessively when wide boards are used, to the extent that a gap appears between tongue and groove. Similar boards fixed vertically also allow the water to leak round the tongues even when no shrinkage has taken place. Plastics planks of the same design principle, while suffering no moisture content movement, have greater longitudinal thermal expansion, which can result in them springing out of their fastenings. Those traditional claddings—tile hanging and slate hanging—are woefully inefficient at keeping out wind, and where wind gets so too does moisture. The United Nations building in New York gave architects one of the sharpest lessons—the fact that wind striking the face of a wide building must rise and carry the rain with it (Fig. 7.1).

*Fig. 7.1. Use of excessively damp boarding results in excessive shrinkage as the wood dries out, the nominal thickness of the boarding giving a largely misleading idea of the actual barrier to rain and wind which the tongues give.*

Ineffective tying of cladding to structure, whether in design or workmanship, has resulted in expensive and dangerous failures, as has inadequate provision for differential expansion and contraction. Early applications of glass as apron panels in curtain walling did not always allow for exceptional expansion, resulting in shattering of the glass, a risk now well known and catered for in design, usually in the form of seal at edges. That reliable and well-accepted cladding, facing brickwork, has been the loser in a differential movement battle with reinforced concrete frames where the latter have contracted as moisture dried out while the bricks laid fresh from the kiln have expanded. The brick infill being cut tight to the framing has become squeezed resulting in outward movement to the destruction of the panel ties, if any, and development of dangerous bulges.

Ties are a major problem in that the safety of the cladding may rely on them but, through inadequate specification or fixing, they may fail to hold it in place. A well-known contracting/development company had such a failure on one of its own buildings, costing £40 000 in remedial measures, and this despite intensive study of tying methods before erection. An architect specified cast copper ties to be inserted in the backs of medium size concrete facing panels, but after acceptance of a tender agreed to the substitution of galvanised mild steel ties. For transport the mild steel ties were bent flat but for building in they were straightened. It did not occur to the architect that the galvanising—which in any case might have a 'life' of only ten years—would be breached by this double bending. He was fortunate that collapse of the facing did not occur until after expiration of seven years. Apart from the local authority owner's liability to compensation to any pedestrians who might have been injured, there was the inescapable heavy cost of adding nonferrous bolting of all the panels to the structure which they had to do.

Concrete slab joints are so prone to leakage that various systems have been evolved, all capable of being misunderstood. Most of these are excellent when well applied, while some are only satisfactory where vandals with pointed sticks cannot get at the sealing strips. The use of such a system would be an office decision, but the site architect might find himself with a nagging doubt about the permanence of the joints and look for some built-in protective device, at extra cost of course. There remains the worry as to how some of these seals, fillers, etc. are to be replaced in later years as ageing sets in. In supervision one has to be sure that drained joints vertically have the neoprene strips brought over the faces of the horizontal strips which one can scarcely see once the panels have been erected and just hope that rising rain will not leak past. Some doubts may also arise, where pressed metal sills are used, as to whether the wholly hidden bedding will keep out rain in turbulent winds. Insulating strips, however, placed between panels and columns to prevent cold bridges, can sometimes be seen for weeks after fitting before the inner linings are placed.

There are concrete cladding panels which incorporate expanded plastics insulant in the concrete envelope. There can be no proof that the insulant is in the correct position, is of the correct type, of correct thickness and covers the correct area until tests are made with thermocouples on the completed building, but this is too late for the architect to complain and involves an expensive proof system to be authorised. There is one case where the architects have been quite unable to ascertain how rain gets into the concrete framed concrete panelled buildings—enough rain to squirt out as a jet when a hole is cut above the bearing beam. To make matters more trying the water rarely accumulates twice in the same place.

Another problem arises where airborne moisture from within the building can penetrate the inner lining and condense on the inner face of the cladding. There must be thousands of buildings where this ought to be happening if theory and laboratory tests are to be believed. Protection of the outer facing is essential if steel-framed curtain walling has been used. Accumulations of condensate in the cavity, if no drains are provided, cause rust stains and disfigure for years the storey below in addition to weakening the framing.

Breakage of cladding panels or condemnation of faulty panels may result in several weeks' delay and, due to the lapse of time from original delivery, all the original aggregate or other facing material may be used up, so replacement panels may be markedly different in appearance. This emphasises the need to ensure that the builders check all panels on delivery and store them and handle them to avoid all possible damage.

Inquests on buildings which have collapsed have disclosed many appalling lapses from design principles, in casting units and in site erection. Extended hook-ended reinforcement in floor slabs intended to be married with exposed hooks in the structural frame have been so mis-shapen as to make this impossible. When the building collapsed, all agreed that it was a miracle it ever stood up. No one during erection had the initiative to stop the work and have remedial action taken, as an inspecting architect would be expected to do if he were to avoid a claim for negligence after collapse.

The different mastics, whether adhesives, sealants or fillers, are difficult enough to know and identify without the further confusion of brand names being added. Some are strips or ribbons, some are fluid, some paste mastic and some gun-applied. Some are liable to drip in warm weather, some bleed into porous materials causing staining unless precautions are taken. Some are only available in black, some grey, some have a choice of colours and one cannot remember whether the different colours indicate different uses. Some very old mastics still serve very well, including white lead paste, red lead, putty and bitumen compounds, but all have their limitations and faults if used the wrong way.

Surface blemishes from scaffolding, mastics, paints and blows must be guarded against, yet builders are often quite reckless. This should only be the situation where the specification, bills and supervising architect all fail to lay the responsibility clearly on the builder. Yet if staining does result and cannot be rectified despite the builder's best efforts the client is saddled permanently with a fault for which no money can compensate. Some 'cures' can make faults worse. Wire brushing a facing brick to remove mortar splashes can tear the face away and worsen the disfigurement but this treatment would in any case be useless on a deeply textured brick. Experiment on a similar brick not used in the structure is a necessary first course. Often the makers of the facing, be it concrete, enamelled panel, GRP or other material, can suggest a treatment; if not perhaps the makers of the material causing the stain know the answer. Then there is always the Building Research Establishment who have a great number of problems from the naïve to the most perplexing, brought to them for solution. Quick action which does not allow time to seek advice may be needed. A dribble of bitumen from flat roofing work on stone will certainly stain: if a solvent is immediately applied the bitumen becomes spread and absorbed into the stone whereas if left to harden most of it can be picked off with quite a small stain left for removal by dry treatment.

The practice of slurrying ashlar stone facing with lime is another that has been largely dropped. It was said to protect the face and assist in rubbing down. The labour of rubbing down and the need for operatives to wear protective masks probably had a lot to do with it as it has affected other practices which were hazardous to health. The old practice however had the merit that minor defects in laying the stone could be disguised in rubbing down; now one must have the stones laid correctly in the first place.

Rendering can be included in claddings. The common renderings of trowelled cement and sand, roughcast and pebble or spar dashing generally suffered from the base coat being trowelled too much, resulting in the laitance being brought to the surface to the detriment of the inner thickness, resulting in crazing. Thrown-on rendering has overcome this even when smoothed by trowel, but in matching old surfaces the old practices have to be followed. Much of the old troubles, however, are thought to have been due to using too much Portland cement in the mix, and this is now avoided by using lime/cement/sand mixes varying in proportions according to the time of the year, but generally being about 1:1:6. In using renderings it has to be borne in mind that some bricks give a poor base, having a greasy nature, or they may be prone to efflorescence. Where these must be used, it is necessary to have grooved bricks or meet the cost of providing a mechanical key like expanded metal lathing. Most builders seem quite confident in applying renderings to such bricks after they have been brushed with a bonding coat of one of the well-advertised materials which so often turn the improbable into the practicable nowadays.

Plastics-bound renderings, usually applied by specialists, seem to be the most reliable, and these are cases where the inspecting architect may well feel he ought not to criticise practices but only the finished results and then rely on the guarantee of reputable companies for any genuine faults which may appear. If the physics and chemistry are not fully understood by the architect he could invite failure in insisting on having the work done his way and not the specialists' way.

# CHAPTER 8

# *Carpenter and Joiner*

Specifications commonly name the kinds of softwoods and hardwoods which may be used. The wide variety of species, sources and qualities makes identification of even a proportion of them a task for an expert with a microscope and reference books, so how can an inspecting architect possibly know at a glance what he ought to reject as not being from an approved source, for instance? As to softwoods there is fortunately little probability that timber from a reputable merchant will be other than good material of one of the approved species, but old stock can be infected with woodworm and wet rot with, in some areas, the additional possibility of beetle attack. There are rare cases where merchants of highest standing can be caught quite innocently. One firm of merchants and joinery makers of high standing selected from their stock English oak for about 2000 window sills. After about a year there were reports of small flies appearing which the makers found had hatched out of the apparently excellent oak. At their own cost they replaced all the sills. This came to light after the expiration of the defects liability period, so had the wood been supplied by a less high-principled company the architect would have been faced with the very difficult problem of finding where the flies came from and having to recommend the clients to take legal advice which, even after court action, could have left them very much out of pocket, the time absorbed being unremunerated. If the machinist working the oak did not discern the holes where the eggs were lying, a visiting architect could not expect to see them or understand their significance. Impregnation against pests is not customary with hardwoods though there is a growing demand for treatment of softwoods.

Waney edges on carcassing timber seldom have any serious effect on strength but may make difficulties in fixing plasterboard. Shakes are another matter, as are large loose knots, both affecting bending strength.

Stress grading of timber which was greeted with great enthusiasm some years ago is an excellent principle but is almost impossible to apply in practice, though at least one merchant has developed a computerised method of grading. If anything less than the highest grade is required, the architect is bound to find it impossible to condemn the timber unless it carries a warranty from the merchant. Instead he may find that the merchant will not bother to stress grade the timber but will select and send only that which is entirely free of objectionable blemishes—better than that required maybe but cheaper for him.

Another defect is members which are not straight. A floor joist in twist is pushed into line by the strutting, but a humped joist cannot be straightened without a lot of trouble, even then relying on strutting and flooring to keep it right. As the wood dries out, slackening the strutting, the hump is likely to return.

Joist ends cut on to wood plates in walls are the simplest way of getting a correct line, but this has many disadvantages, such as shrinkage of the plate, open joints in the beam filling and exposing plate and joist ends to moisture when in an external wall. In thousands of buildings there is no bad result but the principle is poor. In some areas a steel flat plate was used, which was tarred and sanded, but it presented difficulties in fixing the joists. Joist hangers have largely taken over but these need watching for if the builder is not to cut each joist to suit the level of its hanger the resultant floor plane is likely to be somewhat undulating. If on the other hand the builder wisely fixes all the hangers to a batten at a level which enables the bricklayers to bed at exactly the correct level (Fig. 8.1), someone has to see that the bricklayers have gone to the extra trouble to chop in mortar under every flange, which cannot be seen after the next course is laid. In party walls use of joist hangers ensures that the Building Inspector can be happy that the joist ends from the adjoining floors have at least the minimum spacing. In one house surveyed because of the peculiar behaviour of the floor, some of the joists were found to be bearing on the walls only between $\frac{1}{2}$ in/12 mm and 1 in/25 mm, the sort of shoddy work that could not be hidden if hangers had been used. The builder probably saved a foot length on every joist by this sharp trick.

Joist ends built into or touching solid external walls should have their ends treated with preservative, and this applies even to wood delivered impregnated, for impregnation seldom penetrates to the core. This can be important but is often avoided because (*a*) the wood is too wet to take the oil-base preservative, and (*b*) the carpenter does not want to wait for a painter to apply the preservative after cutting to length, nor does he want to get splashed with wet preservative as he drives in the nails. Where impregnated joists are used, every cut made by electrician, plumber or other should be followed by the man with the preservative brush.

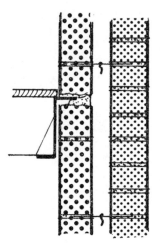

*Fig.* 8.1.    *The convenience of bedding joist hangers in bed joints has often to be forgone. They must be fully bedded and not as shown.*

Excessively high moisture content is more likely to develop on site due to lack of protection than in the merchant's yard, and this may only reach an acceptable level after the building is occupied. It has been said that a house of traditional construction requires a year to enable woodwork to come down to 10–12 per cent moisture content. Moisture content really needs an instrument for measurement, and fortunately these are now quite cheap and have other uses. The wetter a structural member is the more it will shrink as the moisture content is reduced; major shrinkage occurs in girth, but there is slight shrinkage in length also. Softwood tongued and grooved flooring is sometimes laid so wet that when it dries out the shrinkage exposes the full width of the tongue if the flooring has been nailed. Such flooring ought not to be fixed, and precept requires that it be cut to length, turned face down and allowed to dry before nailing at the last possible moment. This practice is not popular as there is some risk of accident, but if this is not adopted, the flooring should only be in narrow widths where the relative shrinkage is proportionately reduced. Flooring grade chipboard does not suffer from this shortcoming, but traps for access to electrical drops are not nearly so easy to form. One very influential housing authority is reported to refuse to allow chipboard to be used.

Scantlings of joists, rafters, purlins (Fig. 8.2), etc. listed in the

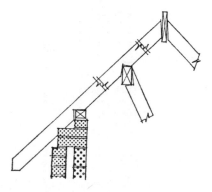

*Fig. 8.2.  Extensive use of trussed rafters supplied made up gives carpenters little practice in traditional roof framing, with the results which are sketched here where, due to poor contact between faces, most of the stresses are necessarily being taken by the nailing alone. Wood wedges are sometimes hammered in to make good defective cuts.*

Building Regulations are considerably smaller than traditional sizes (at least in the first third of this century, the Victorians being prodigal), so the loads individually taken are higher. As the tables set out the centres, the builder should not exceed them, but a thoughtful builder can quite easily save a joist here and there in a house by stretching the fixing centres. The shallower the joist depth the less effective herringbone strutting can be in making a number of joists share a load, apart from the slackening caused by shrinkage which cannot generally be prevented, so the inspecting architect may feel this type should be restricted to deep joists, requiring solid strutting to shallow joists. Unless strutting is effective joists deflect individually with destructive effects on the ceiling plaster underneath. An interesting problem arises, where, in crosswall or similar constructions, an upper floor front apron frame is attached to the first floor joists for resistance to twisting. This can only be done when both are unloaded so both later deflect, even if the apron framing is cambered to allow for this. The consequence is that the nearest floor joist to the apron takes some of the apron loading which it is not designed to do. Effective strutting can share this load on two joists at least, but calculation of the load would be better avoided.

Scantlings reduced to the minimum by calculation may overlook the habits of those trades whose activities follow the carpenter, in the main the plumber and the electrician. These trades appear to have no hesitation in notching joists without regard to the effect on strength. In housing work the electrician can often co-operate by drilling through joists near the neutral axis but a plumber can seldom do this (Fig. 8.3). It follows that the architect should stress

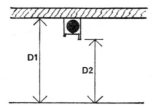

Fig. 8.3.   *The structural depth has become $D_2$ as the result of the notching. This may not matter near the bearings.*

to the builder, plumber and electrician that any structural timber weakened by unnecessarily deep cutting (which may be deeper than the notching) will require that member and others similarly affected to be replaced at the builder's cost. In one instance the architect discussed with the plumber how he would run a heating pipe in the thickness of a wood joist floor, and asked the plumber to pass a certain trimmer before turning the pipe parallel with it. This the plumber failed to do because, he said, it was easier for him to notch the trimmer! So the builder had to put in a new trimmer, at the plumber's expense one hopes.

Traditional connections of joists to trimmers and trimming joists are seldom considered necessary now, but this must be decided by the architect considering what loads have to be transferred. Gang-plate nailing and joist hangers may be quite strong enough whatever the specification may have called for, while half-housing for simple trimming for small rooflights should suffice, but even this takes longer than fixing by mechanical means—but it can be done without waiting for the metal parts. Even reliance on 6 in/150 mm nails may be enough if there is no chance of the two members moving apart.

Another small change in custom is specification of 1½ in/38 mm joists as an economy measure. This is in order if no other fixings are affected but difficulty may be experienced by the builder in obtaining joist hangers for this thickness, and his plasterer may be troubled because he has difficulty in fixing plasterboard to 1½ in/ 38 mm joists when the recommendation is to nail these boards ¾ in/19 mm from the edges; so at best the plasterer can only drive the nails skew to get any fixing. Heading joints of floorboards present the same problem but not so acutely, so many builders do not think 1½ in/38 mm thickness floor or roof joists are practicable and so they use 2 in/50 mm types, but not free—the cost had been foreseen but that is no reason why the builder should not demonstrate to the architect the fixing difficulty and extract from him an instruction to cover the extra cost which the architect would have to be hard to resist.

Softwood for joinery should be inspected for freedom from large knots, splits and any other obvious defects, and it should be machined smooth and square, although it is not necessary to smooth all faces, for a sawn-finish back to a door frame in a plastered partition does no harm and is in fact common in some parts of the UK. It is not even necessary that a joinery member shall be as straight as a straightedge, so long as it can be made straight in use, as an architrave can but a mullion cannot.

Much softwood joinery ought not to be accepted because of the grossly inadequate attention paid to finish. Cutter marks from spindles in plane surfaces and simple mouldings are all too common, even to the extent of skipping over coarse saw cuts, and these should be condemned. Only in the most expensive work is a hand finish expected, but that is no reason for accepting bad material in low cost contracts. The best results are obtained from hand moulded methods, but these call for craftsmen.

Joinery being 'second-fixing', in the main the moisture content should be lower than is common for structural work, but it will still absorb moisture from other materials. Wood framed stairs come half way, usually being fixed before the joinery trims and frames, and so are fixed in wetter buildings and are likely to show more shrinkage than other joinery. Priming is specified for softwood before delivery, but with what object is not clear, for it is quite unable to protect the wood from entry of moisture. Shrinkage must be expected unless the building is all prefabricated in warm workshops, erected in dry weather and requires no wet trades after erection and glazing. In these conditions the recommended 12 per cent moisture content for wood in centrally heated buildings is reasonable as the joinery should not be able to absorb moisture from the building and is most unlikely to dry out to below 10 per cent at any time, and so is virtually shrinkage free.

Manufactured joinery varies greatly in quality but in general one gets what one pays for, though this is not the unvarying rule. So the architect has to see that deliveries are up to the standard he expects from that maker or groups of makers. The fact that a pattern of fitting is an EJMA standard does not mean that opening lights will not bind, doors will not need easing and drawers will not have so much play that they jam in their recesses. Nor does it mean that plywood panels will be sanded smooth and have no uncemented plies.

Flush doors are another item with a very wide range in quality. Those relying on British Standard may reasonably assume that a door offered having a skeleton core will be satisfactory in appearance, but only if the architect is not perturbed to see the skeleton layout showing through the facing panels. On the other hand he can buy at much the same price a hollow framed door with similar faces which, having quite a different core, does not show its construction through the facings (Fig. 8.4). This is quite apparent as one looks at buildings, but this defect also shows up in solid core flush doors because the battenboard core is of low quality. The choice is one made in the office but the site architect may decide that the quality delivered, even though of the construction selected, is unsuitable. However, he may be unaware of this until a door is painted or polished because the essential reflection of light is not possible earlier.

Doors required to have $\frac{1}{2}$ hour and 1 hour fire resistance are demanded increasingly. As the former are $1\frac{3}{4}$ in/44 mm thick and the latter $2\frac{1}{4}$ in/57 mm thick, identification may be fairly easy if all other doors are either $1\frac{7}{8}$ in/47 mm or $1\frac{5}{8}$ in/41 mm thick, but $1\frac{3}{4}$ in/44 mm thickness is not uncommon for unclassified flush doors. The obvious clue is comparative weight, but if the builder fits an unclassified door in an opening required to have half-hour fire resistance, with the result that fire spreads, it will be the architect who takes the blame for failure to comply. He must see too that such doors have three hinges and the correct kind of door stop on the frame, in addition to fitting of an approved type of fastening and self-closing device.

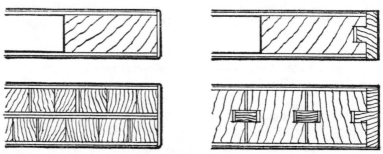

*Fig. 8.4.     The upper plans represent hollow core doors having wood veneered faces on plywood or hardboard. The left hand one has a veneer-lipped edge only, while the right hand one has solid lipping which can be shot by the carpenter to fit the door frame. The lower plans show solid core doors, in the right hand example the wood veneer being brought over the edge of the solid lipping which avoids the break in grain and maybe colour to be expected of the lipping of the hollow core door. Not all door makers mask the solid lipping with the veneer on solid core doors. Joinery doors are usually shot to the frame, with their long edges slightly bevelled towards the stops, but this is obviously not possible with veneered edges.*

Mitre cutting and scribing are simple operations which are often badly done. Softwood with a high moisture content used for architraves shrink in the width, so what starts off as a neat mitre at the head finishes as a thin V joint (Fig. 8.5). Skirtings are seldom scribed to floors but where these are of boards it should not be omitted, though again shrinkage of the softwood usually results in a considerable gap, hence the gaining popularity of hardboard skirtings and architraves which do not move nearly so much as softwood. Scribing a mould to a brick reveal around a window or door frame is possible to do well only when the bricks are smooth faced and well built, yet the effort has to be made when frames are fitted after the openings have been formed. Some architects specify quadrant moulds for this situation, which are the least suitable sections. Softwood or hardwood skirtings cannot conform to uneven plaster surfaces so it is pointless to blame the carpenter where gaps are seen behind skirtings—a situation which hardboard skirtings can overcome, being fixed by hard steel nails wherever a gap appears. It is also impossible to fix architraves to uneven plaster at door linings:

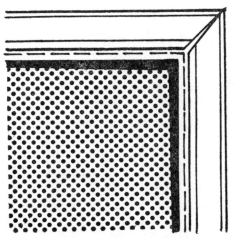

*Fig. 8.5. Shrinkage of architrave after fixing results in the V at the mitre. The door is shown as it is often hung, with wide fit to frame instead of about $\frac{1}{16}$ in/2·5 mm but this could be due to a bad frame badly fixed out of plumb and square.*

either the plasterer should put his work right or the painter must mask the defect with stopping (Fig. 8.6).

Identification of hardwoods in the raw often calls for a fine knowledge of timbers. It is not easy to tell Sapele mahogany from straight-grained Lagos in the solid. It is also difficult to separate Obeche from Agba, yet not difficult to sort West African Walnut from European and Australian Walnuts or American Black Walnut. Fortunately on site this problem does not often arise as the more characterful woods are usually specialist items, like veneered and solid fittings. Nevertheless some of these need watching, for birch tastefully stained can at a quick glance be mistaken for mahogany, but not on close examination. There are similarities in Honduras Mahogany, rotary cut Lagos Mahogany and Israeli Cedar but conversion methods must be understood to know when a veneer has been

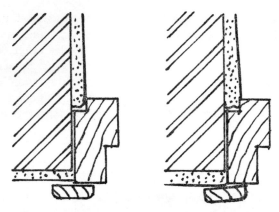

*Fig. 8.6. Conditions derived from the plasterer which the joiner cannot overcome in fixing the architraves. The sketches also show the problem presented to the plasterer by rebating the frame for plaster: in the left hand reveal the plaster rebate is wider than the plasterer needs, while in the right hand reveal he has brought out the plaster to fill the rebate resulting in a splayed reveal.*

rotary cut and when flat cut, the effects being quite different when the latter is radially cut.This is seen best in the fleck of figured English Oak and sheen of Fiddle-back Sycamore, while the former is seen in plywood made with Columbian Pine, Birch, Japanese Oak and Alder.

Likenesses in timbers are so close that any unusual hardwood specified has to be well known for it to be recognised; even so in some timbers, like Muhuhu, samples can be markedly different in colour, but this may not be important if the timber used is of the colour and character wanted. Substitution is no doubt common but unlikely to occur to the extent of supplying Afrormosia when Utile was required, the colours being different. Similarly so-called Rhodesian Teak (Iroko) would not be substituted for Burma Teak because the former, an excellent timber, has quite a different colour from genuine Teak. The position is not made easier by some merchants acquiring a flitch of veneers with an unusual character of a well-known wood giving it a new name.

Architects have an established habit of specifying '3-ply' panels when they should not. Plywood 6 mm in thickness may be of 3-ply, 4-ply, 5-ply and perhaps 6-ply, but if it is 3-ply it is probably of Columbian Pine, Swedish Pine or something similar which is not suitable for veneering on, because the wild grain shows through the veneer, and it is equally unsuitable for painting. Plywood ought to be specified by thickness and face veneer or by use as 'for painting', but if it is specified 'for polishing or staining' then the kind of veneer must again be identified. The number of plies is not important. What is important is the kind of glueing or cementing and this is very difficult to tell on site. For indoor use no problems are likely to arise, except with the cheapest 'tea-chest' plywood of foreign origin, but for outdoor use WBP quality is essential. Even so the architect relying on this specification finds trouble, for the veneers at their edges have been known to rot, leaving the resin cement films as frills, which can be reduced by sealing the edges with paint. Defects in plywoods are split veneers, blistered veneers and knots. The first two should not be found on a site, but the last cannot always be avoided in Birch and Alder plywood, because the small-girth trunks naturally have vestiges of branches. Most blemishes in the face plies are cut out and plugged with similar wood during manufacture but in Birch and Alder the small knots are often left, being tight, and in staining and polishing are considered decorative. The architect must be clear what he wants and what it is reasonable to expect to see on site.

Blockboards, battenboards and laminboards are of distinctive construction and are not necessarily superior to plywoods but the finest work would employ laminboard and the cheapest battenboard, though whether the difference could be detected in the finished work depends a lot on selection of board. While WBP quality is common in plywoods, there is some scarcity of similar quality in the blockboard family, which can result in long delays in delivery.

Cabinet work delivered to site having a veneer finish not seen in construction in a workshop may be found to be veneered chipboard when the architect expected to see one of the blockboard family, and he might be inclined to condemn it straight away. This could be rash as the question is whether the material is essentially suitable for the use to which it is to be put. As most of the mass-produced cabinet work is based on chipboard in preference to blockboard nowadays, the architect has to find that chipboard will fail in use where blockboard or something similar would not fail. The smaller shrinkage movement due to moisture content in chipboard is in its favour, while the absence of long fibres is against it, as is its poor screw-holding, although there are ways of overcoming this handicap cheaply. Much of the shrinkage experienced in cased stairs would be avoided if chipboard were used for treads and risers when the correct details are adopted. Chipboard is still regarded as the 'poor relation' of the blockboard and plywood industry, but with some injustice. Carpenters and joiners using hand tools dislike chipboard, however, because it quickly takes the cutting edges off, but the same can be said of teak.

Timber used externally must be allowed to expand and contract with changing moisture content, which is why boarding should be fixed with one nail or screw only in its width. Curling of boards is then to be expected as the outer face dries and shrinks while the inner face remains slightly damp, the only way of keeping the curling under control being to use a fixing system which keeps both edges under restraint (Fig. 8.7). If feather-edge boards are nailed

*Fig.* 8.7.   *Weatherboarding free to expand and contract, held in position but not double-nailed, which could cause splitting.*

near their thin edges the thick edges will curl outwards, but if they are nailed through the thicker part just beyond the overlap with the thin board below, the thick part is held by the nails and the thinner part by the covering board. This exposes the nails to the weather, hence the temptation to nail the board where covered. This calls for either galvanised or composition nails, and this is particularly important where Western Red Cedar is used, otherwise staining will be very obvious.

There is a wide choice of metals for fixing carpentry and joinery, but non-ferrous nails and screws are not only softer but generally more expensive than steel and are not always easy to obtain. Nevertheless screws used in positions exposed to dampness should not rust. The situation might occur where cast iron hinges are used but are fixed with steel screws in creosoted timber, the consequence being that the screws rust not only on the surface but in the timber. Yet this is not a position where non-ferrous screws should be used, so the only sensible solution is to see that protected steel screws are used, either galvanised or sherardised. It might of course be argued that brass hinges should have been specified, and this might be correct, and brass screws would naturally be used, but occasionally one finds that steel screws have been slipped in because there were no brass ones handy. Non-ferrous or stainless steel screws are always used in polished wood.

Length of fixing is also of consequence. A nail should be twice as long as the thickness of the member it is fixing, and this rule can also be applied to screws, although less rigidly. Type of nail varies with situation, a 'cut' nail commonly being used to fix to walls, an 'oval' nail for joinery, a 'flooring brad' or 'lost-head brad' for flooring, though sometimes small cut nails are still used, but this use should be discouraged because if the board has to be taken up this type of nail splits it, while a flooring or lost-head brad can be driven or pulled through. In small fillets, coppered steel lost-head brads or panel pins are used, while in carpentry wire nails, whose thicknesses do not seem now to be available in the former large variety, are used rather more than cut nails. Of screw types the much advertised 'Pozidrive' heads are excellent in preventing damage from the driver slipping, but when painted or polished the heads are so filled that removal by unscrewing is virtually impossible. The better course in this situation is a slot head and cup if countersunk or a raised or domehead screw, but these would only be used if removal is likely to be done frequently. The other argument for using cups with countersunk screws is that, with the wood being drilled for the cup exactly, the cup protects the wood—generally polished hardwood—from injury by the screwdriver.

Aluminium fittings will usually be fixed with aluminium alloy screws, but satin-chrome plated brass screws may be more suitable in being less friable, while bronze finish fittings should also have matching screws. This may not be easy to ensure any more than lacquered brass screws can be found for polished lacquered brass fittings.

The common fault with screw fixing is failure to put the screw in the centre of the hole in a fitting. This is usually due to carelessness because a centre-punch was not used to locate the centre, the screw being put roughly in position then knocked half-way home with a hammer prior to tightening with the screwdriver. On the other hand it may be wisdom as when hinges are fitted to $1\frac{3}{8}$ in/35 mm doors. The wings of the butts are then so narrow that some of the staggered holes come very near the pin. If then the screw is driven square into the door it comes so close to the face of the door as to raise its surface, even to spring the hardboard face off the timber framing. So the wise carpenter puts the screw in on the skew a little. Otherwise, there are few justifiable occasions.

There are also the strange customs of supplying round- or dome-head steel screws only in japanned finish, and coachbolts and screws only in black oxidised finish, and it seems impossible to obtain these finishes on any other types of screw. Japanned finish is not permanent protection from rust, holding the metal rather less well than the oxidised black finish. Coachscrews should have matching washers, but coachbolts, having square shanks under the heads, do not.

Gauge of screw, described by its number, is selected rather arbitrarily in architectural circles, but fixings with countersunk holes dictate the gauge of the screw, although it does not follow that the joiner will use the correct size; he is quite likely to use a size smaller which, under the reduced selection principles being applied in the ironmongery business, means two gauges under, with the result that the screw head has very much reduced bearing on the counter-sunk hole. The correct screw should fill the countersink flush with the body. The number of screws a butt hinge requires varies with maker, being three or four for a 3 in/75 mm butt, for example. As the lesser number is sufficient for practical purposes on lightweight doors, no real harm is done if a fourth hole is left without a screw, but it does look unfinished. Some door linings are of 20 mm thick softwood, which is not enough to take the weight of a heavy door, and this is made worse when the leaf of the butt is housed into the lining. The remedy is to fix to the back of the lining a block of softwood to reinforce the lining which then demands that the screws used are of sufficient length to penetrate well and hold well into the block. Framed grounds to linings serve the same purpose.

# CHAPTER 9

# *Roofer*

## METAL ROOFS

Except in repair work, traditional practices have very largely been abandoned due to the search for cheaper and perhaps quicker ways of using metals. Manufacturing techniques have assisted and encouraged new methods.

Lead is still cast on site for re-use on cathedrals, where creep must be discouraged, and this is not a technique in which the architect is expected to have a greater knowledge than the leadworker, the latter being as surprised and annoyed as the architect if a sheet newly cast proved pervious. Rolled lead in repair work is still sometimes required to be of 2·5 mm thickness on prestige buildings, but this is reduced to 0·75 mm in cheap work. The latter has so little resistance to thermal movement that its life in roofing is likely to be quite short, though it will be more lasting as flashing while most lasting when cemented to a rigid board which requires a different jointing technique from the traditional, to the extent of using standing welts rather than rolls.

Zinc has been regarded as a poor substitute for lead and its use where cats can get to it has been discouraged. This objection is still valid, although many roofs are inaccessible to cats, but it does suffer from prolonged exposure to a greater extent than lead, so, while the technique of cementing it to rigid boards is a sound use effecting considerable saving, its use is greater in flashings which can be replaced fairly easily when eroded. Its stiffer character responds well to machine bending but causes some difficulty in forming standing welts formed monolithically, the preference being to use cappings.

Copper had a new lease of life when thin rollings became available, and traditional fixing techniques could be used without much alteration, while cementing it to a rigid backing made fixing easier and saved sarking boards, though its use must have regard to other metals which may be in contact with it or receive water from it.

Aluminium has scarcely had a traditional use, much confusion arising from the availability of so many alloys and hardnesses. Sheet roofing ought to be fairly hard, while flashings ought to be soft to allow of dressing, especially on to slate or tile roofing; but this is not so necessary in apron and stepped flashings. Gauges are thin whether cemented to rigid backings or laid over sarking boards. It is not possible for a site architect to check which alloy is being used, but he can apply a gauge to the metal, although burred edges may give a wrong reading. In addition, the differences in gauge are so small that he can easily make a mistake. Metric thickness specification has overcome the confusion caused by the many differing gauges.

In using all metals, a clean base with all nailheads well sunk is essential. Where they are not rigidly backed, separation from the deck by felt of one kind or another just as a separation layer seems well worth while to ensure that there can be no chemical attack from anything in the wood or other deck material. Metals used traditionally should be supplied in the traditional sizes of sheet and should have rolls and drips at the old spacings which have been found from experience to be those most satisfactory, taking account of movement and fixings. Any attempt to improve on tradition using traditional material is likely to lead to failure. It is much better, for instance, in using sheet lead, to have an additional drip rather than eliminate a drip by using an unusually long sheet. It is also unwise to change the form of a roll or expect a technique used with one metal to be successful with another.

Metal roofs are so little used that the ordinary plumber gains little experience in them, except in repair work, so it is often much better to employ specialists in using the metals or to use the metals in ways which give the plumber the least work to do, the carpenter doing the fixing only of the metal-faced wood or fibreboard panels, but leaving the plumber to form the standing welts or caps. In aluminium and copper, specialists supply and fix, working much faster than an unpractised jobbing plumber can be expected to.

Where metal has to be dressed, the risk is always that the metal will be overworked, resulting in thinning in lead and cracking in other metals. Thinning of lead cannot be detected easily, but if the edge can be seen there may be a clue; if so, the plumber must have been unusually careless. In bad cases the plumber may have resorted to soldering or burning to repair his error and this cannot be accepted.

Antagonism is another risk, as might happen if aluminium nails were used for fixing copper or even galvanised steel nails, or copper nails to fix aluminium, but no objection could be made to using either copper or composition nails to fix zinc or lead. Aluminium flashings might be specified for all drips including those for metal windows, which risks the galvanising congeniality failing, resulting in corrosion of both aluminium and steel. Aluminium flashings laid over steel sheeting rails must also be seen to be separated by a sound membrane, some architects being content to rely on short-lived bituminous paint rather than bituminous felt, a labour which would have been avoided by specifying zinc or lead flashings which are congenial to both steel and aluminium. The same trouble could be caused with copper flashings, both arising out of the use for roofing of these two metals with matching flashings.

Corrugated metal roofings require different depths of corrugation according to spans, and this can be misunderstood by assuming that because these are made in certain lengths they will therefore span these lengths without intermediate support. This error would be pointed out by an engineer supplying steel trusses, but the architect using purlins bearing on walls might not discover the error until the builder draws his attention to it—or does not, with the result that sheets sag between purlins.

The common corrugated sheetings are fixed by drive screws or holtbolts, which cannot be omitted either intentionally or by care-lessness, but the most desirable plastics washers and caps can be forgotten. There are also those patent sheetings in aluminium which have secret fixings which could be reduced from the desirable number. Corrugated sheeting is very light and it is for this reason that the architect should be satisfied that the fixing is good, not only of the roofing but of the purlins also, for in some conditions wind suction can lift roofs and fixings off intact. This is a very real risk and not at all easy to combat. It is often necessary to use steel straps attached to purlin and plate and built into the wall several courses down and at frequent intervals, so as to borrow weight from the wall to overcome the uplift of the wind. These anchorages are easily forgotten at the drawing board. Designers of roof trusses give the uplift in the calculation sheets when the appearance of a minus sign should be taken as a warning by the architect, unless this uplift is transferred to a stanchion or reinforced concrete column with bolting down facilities. Every porch and three-sided building has potential for blowing off the roof, the lighter it is the greater the risk in conditions well below hurricane level, because wind under the roof assists the suction above it.

Wind in gusts exerts strong forces and plays unexpected tricks, such as lifting apron flashing in thin lead and aluminium, but there is not much one can do to prevent this.

## TILE ROOFS

Plain tiles were once fixed to 3 in/75 mm gauge, then to $3\frac{1}{2}$ in/89 mm and later to 4 in/100 mm, which is now accepted as standard practice, except of course where a little extension in setting out the battens saves a few thousand tiles. Plain tiles used to be made 11 in × 7 in as well as the current size of $10\frac{1}{2}$ in × $6\frac{1}{2}$ in/267 × 165 mm so in repair work the former size may be encountered, which can only be successfully overcome by stripping the larger size tiles from, say, the top course, replacing these with the smaller tiles and putting the old tiles in the patch area. This expensive course has the advantage that the re-fixed old tiles should have the same colour of aging as the neighbours.

Plain tiles fixed at 4 in/100 mm gauge have a lap, in slate parlance, of barely 2 in/50 mm, allowing for the nail hole. Traditional tile pitch is 40°, at which this lap seems to be satisfactory, but at eaves the architect often requires a considerable 'bell-cast', which reduces this pitch very much, inviting leakage by rain being driven upwards in the joints. If a bell-cast is wanted then it should start from a much steeper main roof to permit use of a 40° pitch at the eaves (Fig. 9.1). The other error is to show the eaves tilting fillet too low— it is usually the top of the fascia—with the result that the eaves undertile droops correctly into the gutter, but the first course of full length tiles rides on the top end of the eaves tile, resulting in a gap between the two courses of tiles at the gutter. This can of course be pointed but it is an error and pointing can be fatal to battens, as can torching, by preventing rainwater from draining away so that it saturates the battens and rots them.

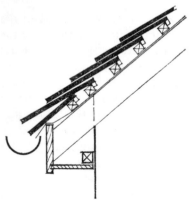

*Fig. 9.1. The fascia ought to be at least 2 in/50 mm higher to prevent the eaves tiles gaping, but if this were done the sarking felt might form a pond behind it. The tiler would protest strongly at this arrangement and would be quite likely to add to the fascia two thicknesses of tile batten to enable him to give a reasonable eaves, without regard to appearance of the bodged fascia. Failure of the architect in his office to detail the eaves can land him in problems like this on site.*

Verge treatment requires the oversailing of the wall face by the tiles by about 1½ in/38 mm, and good practice requires that a raking course of tiles be bedded on the wall to receive the roofing tiles, themselves bedded. There is no real need for the 'undercloak', but it gives a firmer line, though if bargeboards are used the undercloak makes more sense in presenting a continuous line of tiles bearing on the wood; mortar pointing only is sure to fall out, in having no grip to the wood. In this case of course the undercloak tiles have to be nailed rather than bedded. Tiles for the undercloak ought to be 'stringcourse' tiles, *i.e.* not roofing pattern at all, being tiles without camber in either direction which one expects in roofing tiles.

Laced and swept valleys are craftmen's work, an inexperienced tiler soon finding both leading him astray with ever widening spread. The spread must be kept narrow or there is trouble at the ridge. The architect should ensure that the tiler knows what he is doing before he starts work, and see too that the carpenter knows what to provide for him.

In the heyday of twentieth century traditional building, much thought went into roof tiling to design interesting lines and hide otherwise unsightly flashings, so that flashings to upstands which could be seen from the ground were deeply scored and covered with cut roof tiles bedded on, and secret gutters wherever possible.

The effect was to recreate in better form the simple weather protection of earlier buildings where mortar flashings only were used to prevent rain creeping past roof tile abutments, assisted maybe by drip courses in chimneys in particular. These devices are expensive but add great interest to the building, and any intention to repeat them must be discussed with the tiler to make sure that he really understands what is wanted, for he is quite likely to think the architect misguided, as he may well be. There is the case of the well-established architect, responsible for a large estate of terrace houses for one of the New Towns, who detailed the roof tiling very completely around the few chimneys and many rooflights. He was not a little irked to be told by the much respected tiling contractor that these details would leak, might he vary them so as to keep them watertight? The architect responded acidly that a contractor must not criticise an architect's work. So the humbled contractor tiled to details and the roofs leaked.

Plain tiles made traditionally of clay cannot be selected on appearance alone, but there may be a clue in the design, although even here there is no one design. Most tiles are cross-cambered in even thickness and cambered in the length also. This provides drainage space and is generally regarded as the best design. However, there are also excellent tiles which are flat and provide no obvious drainage space but nevertheless they function quite well. The reason for the difference is probably that the former tile was absorbent, and, on becoming saturated, drained from the underside while the flat pattern was harder burned and to a large extent rejected the rain which then fell from its upper surface. Both designs are being superseded by concrete tiles which generally have a cambered upper cross surface only, thus providing drainage space below at the long edges. Tiles submitted for approval should be from a known source, which may be a purely local one, thus allowing one to see their products after they have had many years of use. On breaking, the cross section should show no striations, which would suggest that lamination would occur, and the clay should appear evenly burned in its thickness, not showing dark edges or a pale core. Regular size is not important in plain tile pattern, for one thing hand-made tiles vary in the raw state in density and in moisture content, while position in the kiln can affect rate of burning. In concrete tiles one expects close regularity, and one usually accepts only a make which carries a warranty or preferably a guarantee for a number of years, though guarantees are somewhat unreliable if the makers are a family concern. It is important in accepting any tile to be sure that matching 'fittings' can be supplied at the right time, including valley and bonnet hip tiles, ridge tiles and so on. Ridge tiles, however, may be extruded and be subject to lamination which should be checked.

Nailing of plain tiles used to be every third course; this was extended to every fourth course, then in cheap work every fifth one. It can be supposed that in some work the tiles are only nailed now and then. There is a vogue for aluminium tile nails instead of composition nails; some will question this since moisture and aluminium do not go well together in some alloys, but steel nails must not be allowed. Having specified how often the tiles are to be nailed, the architect should feel tempted on his occasional visits to check that this has been done, using a long stick. It is much better to ask the builder to do the checking while the architect watches, for the tester is certain to push a tile which is not nailed—many of them perhaps—before he finds the first row of nailed tiles, after which he can test with more confidence, but this leaves a very untidy roof with a number of displaced tiles which the builder then has to bring back into line at considerable risk of breakage.

### SINGLE-LAP TILES

Many patterns are extruded and tend to laminate. One maker supplied roofings for thousands of houses even though it was known that in severe frost following damp conditions his tiles would laminate and despite the fact that there was another maker of similar tiles a short distance away whose production methods were superior. The changeover to concrete tiles carrying guarantees must be reducing the numbers of dubious clay tiles, but not all concrete tiles are of equal quality, the most troublesome question being how long the colour will last. Some makers apply naturally coloured granules to the exposed surface and can therefore guarantee colour as well as length of service. In these also the availability of 'fittings' is important, though one does not expect single-lap tiles to be used on roofs requiring much cutting. Special valley tiles are available which, being visible from the ground, must be seen to match the roofing.

Some tiles are designed with weather traps to suit them for flat pitches while others rely on width for the same purpose. Some can be varied in gauge while others cannot, though those without weather traps impose no obvious restriction. All these points influence the choice when the builder is required to submit samples, and the design of roof, pitch and aspect have to be kept in mind, in that some makers of pantiles make right- and left-hand patterns so that the close long edges can be made to receive the prevailing wind on both slopes of one ridge roof. Wind effects seldom cause troubles with any kind of tiled roof where the designer has not insisted on using very flat pitches. Unfortunately some makers encourage architects in this, guaranteeing their tiles to be weatherproof at ever lower slopes, but this results in strong winds lifting them and causing them to rattle, for which the cure is thorough bedding of the top course with the ridge tiles. This complaint may not come to light until long after the roof is finished. It seems likely that there must be a limit to the length of roof slope on which this restraint can be effective.

Pantile and Double-Roman types of tile must have the hollows filled at eaves, some of these being available with closures incorporated in the tiles. The alternative of bedding slips of plain tiles in the hollows seems to work fairly well and looks more interesting, but this would not be the best maintenance-free choice. Verge treatment seems best treated by plain-tile undercloak, but as this is a weak point, parapets are safer though much more expensive. Choice of single-lap tiles is therefore wide and carries many considerations, in weather protection, flashing, verges and eaves. Among the considerations may be how to fix some patterns where cutting is necessary at chimneys, ridges, dormers, etc. It is curious how the catalogues of the makers of single-lap tiles evade this point so often in the illustrations, as if one could always have a full tile downslope from an upstand. This is rarely possible, so the cut tiles must be bedded on mortar preferably on expanded metal on the softwood board, the cover flashing holding it down.

The same treatment must be adopted at ridges where full tiles cannot be used and, where pantiles or Double-Roman types of tiles have been chosen, the hollows have to be filled, there being no pattern available with a suitable upstand to meet the ridge tile. These hollows are best filled with tile slips in mortar, as mass mortar alone is likely to shrink and fall out. A careless tiler can disfigure a roof by slopping mortar on the tiling at ridge, hip and valley.

All single-lap tiles other than the 'slate' type should be set out on the eaves by the tiler before he starts fixing to make sure the verges are going to work out correctly. Obviously on a simple 'ridge' roof the verges at each end ought to overhang the same distance, but if this appears to be excessive the tiler can usually tighten or loosen the horizontal measure to improve it slightly; traditional-pattern pantiles offer the greatest freedom for adjustment. Using 'slate'-type tiles, verge adjustment can be made easily by cutting on the inner edges—this is easy in principle but a ragged edge often results. As with plain tiles, the perpends must be seen to be one above the other in alternate courses from eaves to ridge; wandering perpends cannot be tolerated.

Whatever pattern of tile is approved, it is essential to see that the maker's fixing directions are followed, for failure to adhere to these, whether by architect's instruction or builder's whim, deprives a guarantee of most of its force.

A roof covering neither of tile nor honest slate but which has proved its merits is made of asbestos cement, mostly used in diagonal pattern and in outrageous colours, but also made as simulation slates in grey and grey-blue. These are so light that risk of lifting in wind is considerable but the slate patterns are safer in this respect than the diagonal type which have additional invert nailing to prevent them from rising. Beyond ensuring that fixing is to specification, including gauge, there is not much that can go amiss. There is risk of wind catching verges, where barge board treatment covering the tile or slate edges can prevent this, preferably with zinc or lead cover flashing held with tingles.

## SLATING

Slates can be deceptive in that common slates can appear to be thoroughly weather-proof but be found in the immersion test to be absorbent, water rising well above the surface. There are also slates which soften in exposure, an accusation which used to be applied to Belgian output which had a distinctly blue colour. Smoothness of surface is another questionable clue to quality; in all, the only safe course is to find out where the slates are quarried and where they have been used.

One of the exasperations of using slates is that, in small jobs, the correct size of slate is suddenly not available and another size has to be accepted. It is generally supposed that size of slate is controlled by acceptable lap, but in flat pitches the width of slate is just as important and maybe more so, and therefore acceptance of a small standard size slate having the same lap but less width could be wrong. In this connection one has also the dilemma of which is the better method of nailing—centre or top. This is not likely to matter much except that top nailing requires a slate longer by 1 in/25 mm, but this may be highly desirable where slates are chosen which are wider than they are long.

Nails for fixing must be of a quality which can be cut easily by the slater's knife when he has to replace a broken one, so they must be of composition metal or soft aluminium alloy. Slates are much more brittle than clay or concrete tiles and suffer more when other trades clamber over the roofs to fix telephone lines and aerial masts, etc. While one hopes that this can be avoided, a little forward planning should enable them to be put up before the roof is slated. This however cannot be done for the plumber, who must fix flashings, but plumbers are much more accustomed to having roof ladders provided than are telephone linesmen and aerial fixers. If other trades are to follow the plumber, it is necessary to see that the roof ladders are kept on site and are used, by ridge and hip fixers as well.

## ASPHALT AND BUILT-UP ROOFINGS

There are two if not three kinds of asphalt for roofing—'rock' or 'lake' asphalt, limestone and unidentifiable. 'Rock' and 'lake' are natural products, while 'limestone' is a composition of bituminous binder with limestone aggregate, and all are supplied in cakes, being one or the other British Standard specification number; if they do not carry a number then they are not to British Standard. That is the point of the 'unidentifiable' kind, also supplied in cakes but largely composed of recovered asphalt from roofs which required renewal; this may be composed of both 'rock' and 'limestone' asphalts and so cannot satisfy any British Standard. There is so much of this material about that it would be wasteful to throw it away, but the architect, having specified a BS asphalt of one kind or another, must watch that he is not fobbed off with an inferior material. This of course raises the question as to whether the substitute material is in fact inferior. If 'rock' and 'limestone' asphalts were not compatible this could be understood. Both kinds of BS asphalts are compounded specifically for roofing, but there can be no doubt that the 'substitute' material is also carefully compounded for exactly the same use. Asphalting specialists will usually give a useful guarantee of freedom from failure of material and labour in application which, in the case of the well-known companies (which use both BS varieties according to the choice of the orderers), is valuable to a client, but so will the layer offering 'substitute' material, who will not be one of the well-known users of the BS asphalts.

The point of this is that on small jobs there may be a local asphalter who can use one of the three kinds referred to and give a guarantee of service within the limits of his financial capacity and uncertain longevity, while a layer using only a BS material may not be available in the locality. The only way of telling one kind from another, if the BS mark cannot be seen on the cakes, is by analysis; this is worth while if the architect thinks he is being misled by a contractor, either 'main' or 'sub'.

Asphalt boilers are well-known ornaments of a building site and not much attention is paid to their management. The material should be heated only enough to make it workable, yet often it is overheated in the boiler, which drives off desirable oils and makes the stuff too thin, apart from making working uncomfortable. To overcome this a common trick is to add sand to the boiler, so ruining the carefully worked out proportions in the cakes.

Asphalt which is getting too cold to apply tends to craze under the trowel. This can be caused by a cold surface or chilling wind which the layer has to fight in order to use the hot material dumped in front of him. This also happens when marrying new hot asphalt to the previous shift's work, unless the hard edge is softened by a hot iron. An open crack must not be accepted. The joints cannot be hidden but good work makes them inconspicuous.

As sheathing felt is much in use there is some differential movement between asphalt and base, and some details encourage cracking as a result. This can happen where a lead drip at an eaves has an up-turned edge which the asphalt covers. With the lead being fixed and the asphalt movable, there is some risk of the asphalt cracking over the lead upstand.

Makers of sheathing underfelt for asphalt seem to think that it is the architect's business to specify the kind of felt to be used. This seems more than a little doubtful for no one knows better than the asphalter what kind suits asphalt best, a matter on which few architects have practical experience. There has however been considerable trouble where sheathing felt has been laid over screeded woodwool slabs without a vapour barrier, where moisture from a humid room has reached the sheathing felt and condensed there, softening the lime in the screed which in turn has attacked the sheathing felt, resulting in heavy bituminous exudation dropping from the roof. This risk was not known to the asphalters until several cases had arisen, but it is now understood to have been overcome by changing the constitution of the sheathing felt, though use of a vapour barrier is also essential. It is extremely doubtful whether an architect specifying sheathing felt could be aware that he was in fact laying up trouble for himself by naming the wrong kind. It is much better to put the onus on the asphalter, who ought to be a specialist in his craft.

A usual practice is to trowel in sand on the top course, which does no harm but very little good. What will do good is to trowel in light-reflective spar, but the actual coverage is likely to be less than 100 per cent, so it would be better to specify the omission of sand and subsequent application of congenial adhesive for 100 per cent coverage with spar. One has to be careful that any adhesive does not attack the asphalt.

Vertical asphalt has little grip on brick or stone and needs chicken wire or expanded metal lath for mechanical key above about 9 in/ 225 mm which can damage a parapet by preventing it from drying out on two faces. It is odd that, while $\frac{3}{8}$ in/9·5 mm thickness is standard for flat roofs in each layer, vertical work takes only $\frac{1}{4}$ in/ 6 mm per layer, so there is in fact no skimping.

Built-up roofing is well described in the Building Regulations but the choice is apparently wide as to types of material based on bitumen for flat and pitched roofs. The fire protective considerations influence choice and, faced by an unexpected lack of the specified qualities, forces the architect to study the Regulations once again for suitable alternative combinations of qualities, especially when Ext SAA is required.

Blisters caused by moisture rising through the deck can cause failure in both asphalt and built-up roofings, but with the latter being lighter and more flexible the defects show more clearly. Various devices for ventilating moist vapour are available and can only be left out if there is no possibility of moisture rising, which would be the case where the roofing was over a covered passage externally. What the operative may overlook is the need to ventilate the under-surface, both to let air in and to let it out, which the architect should have detailed. It is all very well to note on the drawing that the roofing is to be carried up against walls 6 in/150 mm but not be stuck thereto, and then show an apron flashing brought down to cover it and stuck to the upstand, thereby sealing in the moist air. At eaves and verges the welted edge should also allow air to enter, but the popular use of extruded aluminium trim makes this difficult to do. Where the details at edges do not ventilate, the safe course is surely to specify roofing vents, but these can only be used where they will not be damaged by window cleaners and painters.

Another weakness of this kind of roof is at vertical corners and perforations for pipes. The latter problem has been largely overcome by production of neoprene sleeves which can provide the complete solution to a problem previously overcome only by sheer bulk of bituminous adhesive. The former problem is only partly solved by heat-extensible flashings which can be welded into the roofing. The burning lamp enables the roofer, when using suitable felt, to over-come many small difficulties, but until effective corner pieces are generally used these points are always weaknesses.

The efficiency of adhesion of one layer to another is always in doubt, the technique of brushing on hot bitumen to one layer and following that up with rolling over the next layer pressed down with the feet is too primitive but is often accepted. A roller would not be much better because of the small undulations in the deck. At one time specialists in built-up roofing guaranteed their work for 10 to 20 years, but this safeguard is no longer available, though the well-established companies will accept responsibility should failure occur within a few years. This is one of the problems, for a repair cannot be made until the point of entry of rain can be pinpointed, which is made more difficult by covering the surface of flat roofs with chippings. The architect has to look at every lapped joint and see for himself that adhesive has been squeezed out and the upper layer is tightly fixed to the lower throughout its length, and that what goes for the final layer also applies to the lower layers. He must also look at all pipes rising through the roofing near to walls, for there is rarely enough space between the pipe and the wall for a good weathertight seal to be made, though this is less difficult in asphalt than in built-up roofing. If the pipe can be projected about 12 in/300 mm from the wall, there is a fair chance of working the roofing around it, but anything less—as it usually is—is bound to be weak.

Dampness is the chief enemy of built-up roofing for in the nature of things the roofing must start at the lowest part of a roof laid to falls to which all moisture gravitates. Moisture on the deck and moisture on each succeeding layer combine to give a very poor roof.

The low elasticity of asphalt and bituminous built-up roofings has lent greater weight to the search for more flexible and elastic roofing materials which are now offered in the many plastics materials on offer, some claiming 50 per cent extensibility which would enable expansion joints in concrete roof decks to be bridged without cutting. Dirt and dampness can affect the adhesion of one layer on another at the laps, but these are fewer than in built-up roofing so there is less to supervise, while the omission of chippings for sun-reflection if not fire protection enables damage to be located fairly easily. How well these roofings last has not been proved in the UK but experience is growing, while the fact that none is named in the Building Regulations simply means that approval has to be sought. There have been failures like that on the experimental bungalow built by a well-known company to demonstrate its wares where the plastics roofing was sprayed on and stood up to sun and wind very well and without sign of failure for nearly a year; then it suddenly disintegrated—or so the story goes.

## CORRUGATED AND TROUGHED ROOFINGS

Asbestos cement, galvanised or plastics-coated steel (including bituminous coated), aluminium alloy, plastics and glass materials offer a very considerable range, and although clear plastics and glass may not be regarded as roofings at all, the former are being used for this purpose extensively.

Asbestos cement sheeting if mishandled can be cracked, but this will not be perceptible immediately. When new it is not so brittle as when it has aged, so on site only rough use is likely to damage it—in fact the same sort of misuse as would damage any other corrugated sheeting. Eaves and ridge closure pieces of some kind are available, of which foam plastics are fairly common, but they must be seen to be well compressed by the sheeting so that they cannot be blown out by wind or attacked by birds which sometimes take a fancy to it. Verge treatment is often poor, there being no really satisfactory sections for roofings of the simple 3 in/75 mm and Big-Six or similarly named corrugations, though there are for some of the troughings. This results in the verges being crude in appearance and weak, lacking protection from driving rain which can enter cracks between sheeting and mortar where thermal expansion has created openings. The feature to be aimed at with verges is that the roofing should have an upturn at each end so that, as far as possible, rain is not thrown on to the wall. This requires that the sheeting be set out carefully before commencing fixing.

The architect inspecting the roofing has to be careful he does not damage or displace any fixed roofing, and he has to ensure that he does not become an accident casualty. The ordinary roof ladder is not much help to the unaccustomed architect, whereas a common rung ladder he can manage quite well, vertigo permitting, so it is worth while getting the builder to afford the architect the means to carry out his inspection safely. This applies not only to tile and slate roofing but also to corrugated roofings, particularly those of asbestos cement which are never safe for clambering over, never mind what the fixers do. On woodwool slab decks, also, there should always be walkways after they have been screeded unless the lines of support under can be distinguished. The risk of serious injury is very great, and the slightest stumble can lead to a fall through the roofing.

# CHAPTER 10

# *Water Engineer and Plumber*

An architect commissioned to carry out a job in an unfamiliar area is likely to assume that there will be nothing peculiar in the bye-laws and regulations of the local water undertaking, so he will probably specify and plan as before. This can land him in trouble at a late if not an early stage, when the response of the undertaking to a protest that a requirement is unusual is often that it is all in the booklet, a copy of which he can have for 15p. Searching through these booklets to find out where the differences lie is time consuming and not always enlightening.

Where houses are concerned, the local inspector is a mine of information, but where a major industrial contract is involved there must be preliminary talks in the planning stage when idiosyncrasies should be, but not always are, revealed.

One of the questions asked will be what water pressure is available, with regard to fire fighting and service to high levels. In one contract for a tall building in the Midlands, the local corporation water department assured the architects at the planning stage that pressure was adequate to serve the topmost storey, with reserve for fire fighting. When the contract was well under way the department was asked for confirmation, and the statement came through that, by day, pressure would be available to serve about 50 ft/16 m and at night to serve about 80 ft/25 m. No explanation was forthcoming as to why the architects had been misled originally, nor was there made any apology or offer of contribution to the extra costs the developers had to pay in installing dual pumps, automatic switches and tanks. As hose reels had to be served the installation was more elaborate than usual.

Another point which did not come to light in the early talks was that the department did not approve of water meters in pits, but insisted on the provision of a water meter room with protection from freezing, again at the developer's cost. As work on site had by then started, provision of this space could have been a major problem.

The site architect is therefore well advised to question very closely the water department in the hope of eliciting all the necessary information, and not just some of it. Even so there can be hurdles to be overcome, like the squabble which arose from an architect's wish to avoid poking individual overflow or warning pipes from WWPs of a range of WCs on an outside wall; by connecting up ten overflows into one $1\frac{1}{2}$ in/38 mm common warning pipe, he was able to reduce the disfigurement to two $1\frac{1}{2}$ in/38 mm pipes, believing that this was a rational arrangement. But the water department thought otherwise, threatening to refuse a supply until each of the WWPs had its own separate warning pipe, because that is what the book of rules required. After a number of meetings the inspector relented with the admonition 'Don't do it again' but adding that no objection would have been raised if the proposal had been discussed with him prior to execution.

No service undertaking accepts philosophically an architect's change of mind once the machinery has been set in motion, even if no extra cost is incurred or is paid for by the client. It is quite possible for the architect to agree with the builder that the site office should be placed at a point next to the boundary without realising that this is exactly where the new 6 in/150 mm diameter water main is to enter. This is avoidable where adequate services drawings are prepared, when the builder would have a copy on which the water entry position would be clearly marked. The client may have entered into an agreement for the supply and have exchanged plans showing the entry point, but he may have omitted to send a copy to the architect or builder.

At one time stopvalves controlling water service were often located on private property but now this is most unusual. Its situation must be one where the cover and concrete margin will not become covered with grass or paving material, which suggests that paths are the best positions. It is preferable not to use drives, for any work requiring the water to be cut off can seriously interfere with access to the premises.

The water authority having made a connection extends this to a short distance inside the property line. Where a metered supply has been agreed, it could be argued that any leakages are paid for by the clients so that they are not a matter of concern for the authority.

However, the authority does not look at the subject this way and requires materials and fittings to be of approved qualities and types: if this includes basin and sink taps, considerable delays can be incurred while they are being blemished with the approval stamps. Approval of materials is in fact helpful, although apparently always well behind the times. A demonstration of this occurred in the border country where the authority had to run a temporary 6 in/150 mm main with an expected life of one year and so ran it in mild steel tube. After 6 months, jets of water were seen at a number of points along its length, and after 9 months the wastage was too serious to be borne. This was all due to the aggressive action of the local water. The authority still uses steel tubes, but only with a cement lining, which has been the complete answer. A New Town had services to the buildings run in plastics tubing some years ago, which was economical and satisfactory until the number of perforations which were reported called for an investigation. The result of the investigation was that rats were attacking the pipes. This was stopped, report has it, by the makers adding to the plastics a rat-repellent substance.

Protection from freezing should require water pipes to be 3 ft/1 m below the surface, but this is seldom demanded, though at some risk to the client's interests. Whatever the agreed depth it is important to watch that subsequent earthworks do not reduce this cover to less. This can happen when a road gradient is changed or a drain crosses the route, pushing the water pipe upwards instead of under it, syphons being no detriment to this service.

The point of entry of the rising main within the building is now controlled, usually being stipulated at 18 in/450 mm from the outer wall, which can create problems in casing and routeing, and is in many cases quite pointless. Probably not more strange than the limitation which may be imposed on there being only one draw-off to a drinking water tap at a sink, despite the ready grant of permission to have any number of hose points for gardening. In an argument with one authority, it was stated that there is no evidence that water from a storage cistern is less potable than that from a rising main. Drinking fountains are usually taken off the rising main so some agreement must be reached on these.

The route taken by the rising main must be discussed with the plumber or water engineer for drawings are an inadequate guide, especially where there are a number of other services competing for space. Again freezing is an important consideration which is not overcome simply because the pipe is within the building, for over the Christmas holiday period heat may be turned off for some days. The effectiveness of lagging may be considered, with or without thermostatically controlled electric warming tapes, especially where a pipe crosses a passageway between two buildings down which there is a persistent wind.

At cistern storage level the provision of two cisterns to give the total recommended quantity is common, the cisterns being cross-connected and valved so that either may be emptied for cleaning. Two ball valves are then required, and this, if care is not taken, can lead to water hammer. This can happen when both valves shut off virtually simultaneously, but it is usually avoided by fitting devices to prevent hammer. It can also be avoided by compelling them to close at different levels, which the plumber may not bother about. The other main point is that water should circulate through the cisterns to prevent standing water (Fig. 10.1), as may happen where

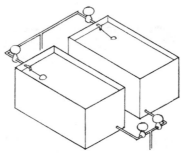

*Fig.* 10.1.   *Desirable arrangement of water entry and outlet to encourage movement of all water in cisterns.*

two cisterns are cross-connected, the ballvalve and all outlets being in one cistern only. A minor point is that the plumber should not fit outlets so low that the deposits of sand and dirt are drained into them.

The position of the warning pipe can lead to freezing of the water in the cistern. It is remarkable how often warning pipes project in an exposed northerly direction, but this is perhaps no odder than the requirement and custom in some parts of the UK of having the expansion pipe discharging not over the cistern but over the roof, being there exposed to winds at the lowest temperatures. As there is usually a choice about where a warning pipe may emerge, this may well be avoidable, but again it is a point that plumbers often ignore. There are protective devices where this cannot be avoided, such as those terminating with a vertical tee, or taking the warning pipe below water level in the cistern.

While on the subject of frost, this is sometimes made more dangerous through running ceiling insulation under the cistern instead of funnelling the house warmth up to its underside.

An airlock in water pipes can be very difficult to move, but fortunately it is less likely to occur in branches from the main than from the down service. Any hump in a pipe traps air which only the force of the water can move. While airlocks are more likely to develop in hot water services than in cold ones (Fig. 10.2), it is essential to

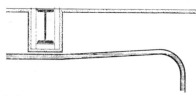

*Fig. 10.2.    The airlock shown is difficult to move if not on main supply with considerable head. This situation could arise where the plumber did not realise that the beam casing would come so much below the steel flange, but it results in a 100 per cent airlock.*

check every horizontal run and every horizontal tee from a vertical pipe to ensure that the plumber has not built in an airlock. An airlock may be temporary, so it does not follow that, because water runs from a draw-off point, be it a tap or WWP, there is no incipient airlock; this can only be proved by draining down the pipes and re-filling, watching to see which outlet fails to discharge water. This test is seldom made until an airlock has been experienced, and the plumber may be quite unaware of it. The device of applying main water pressure to the outlet through a hose moves the lock but is scarcely applicable by a householder to a ballvalve. Some airlocks are partial to the extent that they only reduce the passage of water because the hump is less in height than the pipe diameter, and these airlocks are usually self-correcting in time. The danger of airlocks occurring arises mostly from pipes which sag between their support points, as lead and plastics pipes often do if only held by clips, sagging often being aggravated by softening due to hot water pipes running nearby.

The specified weights and gauges of pipes in an installation must be checked and cut ends should be seen to have been reamed to remove burrs. Special attention may have to be given to the routeing of plastics pipes which cannot be made to conform to small bending radii as can copper, lead or stainless steel, so additional fittings may have to be authorised to enable neat runs to be made.

Tests for leaks must be done before any pipes are enclosed, for a small leak can in time cause dry rot without any evidence of dampness on external faces. Following this the plumber should flush out all new pipework, but this is seldom done when the architect is around. Where drinking water is concerned, however, mere flushing cannot clean the pipes satisfactorily; they should be sterilised by being filled with a compound for this purpose and left to stand for 24 hours. But specifications rarely include this item, and unless the architect directs that it shall be done to his satisfaction it is impossible to be sure that potable water is being delivered. This is a specification requirement for buildings to be occupied by government departments and probably also for most of the large industrial concerns, so it is a matter which should not be ignored.

Handling of sanitary fittings often results in minor damage, while delivery of 'seconds' instead of prime quality goods as quoted is a very tempting way of making a profit. What constitutes 'seconds' is often not at all obvious; it may be that the glaze has not flowed on evenly or there may be a blemish on the undersurface, but it is unlikely that cracked ceramic ware would be delivered knowingly. Distortion can take place in burning, but this may not be evident until a level is applied to back and front of a lavatory basin or a sink. Baths may have the enamel scratched or they may have been placed on a jagged stone, denting them so slightly that the enamel is apparently not cracked but may show in time. WC pans are usually marked 'tested'. Damage may of course occur after fitting so it is pointless to examine all fittings before then so long as the architect can satisfy himself that these are the patterns he selected and obtained quotations for. The absence of identifying marks on sanitary ware makes checking unnecessarily difficult. The builder requires early information on WC pans in particular so it is customary to arrange for samples of all approved items to be sent to site at an early date, bulk deliveries following as the job can use them, so the architect can check the correctness of the sample delivery.

The layout of water services to fittings is seldom drawn out in detail, and so the architect should discuss this with the plumber, who may have no idea of tidy runs and parallel falls. The location of stopcocks must also be considered, sometimes they must be kept well out of the reach of children, or be of the lockshield type to defeat vandals. Ideally the runs to all fittings should be controlled by individual stopcocks, but this can be very extravagant. On the other hand it is parsimonious to provide one stopcock which controls both bathroom and WC.

Pipe sizing is in most jobs largely instinctive, but this is scarcely good enough for the larger installations. Custom gives a good plumbing specialist a good grip of this subject which to the architect may be a chore to be avoided, but it can be important for safety, as in connections to domestic showers where a reduction in flow of cold water to the mixer may result in scalding. This is generally avoidable when no thermostatic control can be afforded by making the shower branch the first of a number, thereby getting preferential service.

After sanitary fittings are connected, all must be tested as to water supply and waste outlet. WC connections give most trouble in that flush pipes not entering squarely into the inlets at the backs can result in uneven flushing of the pans, though this can also result from partial blockage of the rim. Filling time of WWPs varies considerably, being affected by head of water, but occasionally a high-pressure ballvalve may be fitted to a low-pressure supply. Silencing pipes have a habit of getting lost, while another irritating point is that the makers of flush pipes persist in supplying unnecessarily long unions to the WWP, as if all of these were still made of wood or ceramic ware.

Waste pipe runs are critical for single-stack installations as to length and to fall, and so they must be watched; but that other trap—the use of shallow-seal traps instead of 3 in/7 mm seal—has to a large extent gone with the very general adoption of bottle traps. Wastes from urinal ranges are prone to leak where they are quite inaccessible, the fault not being detected for months. The fault may lie of course more at the junctions of the channels, so it is worth checking that these are thoroughly grouted and leak-proof. The adoption of urinal bowls saves a lot of worry.

Wastes for sanitary work can take any of three forms, and it is quite likely that additions to an existing lavatory might have to conform with the two-pipe system, while another might call for one-pipe layout, and new work could be designed as single-stack system, all having differences which the architect must recognise at a glance and which cannot be mixed.

Stack pipes must have their connections in the right sequence in single-stack plumbing, which is sometimes very difficult to contrive when syphonage is a danger, while the incidental labour of sealing around pipes penetrating compartment floors is sometimes overlooked because the plumber has delayed testing out while the bricklayer or carpenter wanted to get on with the ductwork. Another frequent omission is the balloon on top of the vent pipe.

The plumber's work in flashing around chimneys, along parapets and around pipes is virtually inaccessible where pitched roofs are concerned, so much has to be taken on trust. Adequate fixing by wedges of the turn-ins of apron flashings is sometimes scamped, relying instead on the pointing to hold them in place. Incidentally where a cavity gutter extends to the face of the wall immediately above an apron flashing, it seems obvious that the turn-in of the apron flashing should fit below the cavity gutter, but one cannot be sure without looking.

As to rainwater drainage, the large sections of valley and parapet gutters used in industrial work enable good watertight joints to be made in their lengths, with plenty of red lead and hemp or cord for sealing. Some ponding is to be expected if immediate outlets cannot be arranged. A lot of this work is good if it conforms to the prescribed length to the extent of one inch, preferably over than under.

Down pipes are commonly specified to have their joints filled with red lead and hemp or cord, or in some other way, but this is not necessarily good since, if a blockage occurs in the pipe, it may have to be destroyed to clear out the obstruction, whereas if the pipe is only wedged or (if internal) left open, the fixings can be removed and the pipework dismantled.

Plastics eaves gutters on more domestic buildings give a lot of trouble in supervision through inadequacy of support brackets, despite makers' recommendations, and leaking joints. To allow for expansion, the plumber ought to have regard to the temperature at time of fitting the gutters so that, in very cold weather, he gives the minimum lap at the joint in the expectation that in hottest midsummer the expansion of the gutter will take up the rest of the expansion groove; but it may be questioned how many plumbers give this a thought. The consequence is that plastics gutters can be seen bowing between clips through expansion being prevented at the joints. The thermal movement may also have the effect of displacing the joint bedding membrane with the result that a leak develops.

Such defects are unlikely to be observable at the time of erection, but they may show by the end of the defects liability period if by happy chance the architect makes his inspection at a time of heavy rain.

Downpipes for domestic gutters should also be left uncemented, but because the small pipes are easily moved in wind the joints must be wedged, to stop them from rattling. When a blockage occurs, an arrangement where the bottom of the RWP terminates in a shoe discharging over a gulley facilitates clearing, whereas use of a back-entry gully or shoe lets the blockage be washed into the drain.

With asbestos cement rainwater goods, there is some risk of cracked members being fixed, but the initial flexibility of the material, though limited, enables it to be more roughly treated than it would when aged. Collars of down pipes are sometimes cracked by too vigorous wedging.

One further task for the plumber is insulation of pipes, particularly hot pipes. Wrapping felt must cover all parts, though it is often applied slovenly at sharp bends, and it must be tied in place. The split circular foam laggings are probably much tidier and more effective, but they too require special attention at bends. The most important points to watch are of course those where the plumber has difficulty in reaching, such as where a hot pipe rises on an outside wall up to the roof space where even a plumber with long arms has difficulty in pushing the lagging into place, let alone tying it or binding it with adhesive tape, though this is just the point where heat loss or freezing risk is greatest.

There are skills in plumber's work which seldom get exercised today, such as lead-burning and wiped solder joints, and this very lack of practice can result in shoddy work. One looks for thoughtful arrangement of pipes and joints, clean wiped and screwed joints, clips which match the pipes for size and material, smooth unrucked bends in copper and stainless steel tube, and in fact everything done in a craftsmanlike manner which a good plumber ought to exemplify.

# CHAPTER 11

# *Glazing*

The character of glazing putty has changed in recent years. Linseed oil putty may be specified, but a multi-purpose putty may be used which is suitable for metal or wood frames, displacing both red-lead putty and metal-window putty.

While UK-made glass is used in the vast majority of buildings in the UK and in a good many abroad too, there are leanings towards some Continental glasses for quality and easier delivery. Whether this really matters so long as the finished effect is good is a moot point, unless UK glass has been specified. How can one tell, when the glass either comes from merchants or is supplied and fixed by subcontractors? Double-glazing units present no problems, their labels advertising the makers.

Most defects in glass can be seen easily and are unlikely to be manufacturing faults. Most are caused in handling, by scratching one sheet over another or chipping in resting a sheet on a metal edge. The more subtle fault is seen in 'sheet' glass where the wrong face is used externally, the smoother or more even face being exposed to the weather. Manufacturing faults like bubbles cannot be accepted in 'glazing' quality, but some ripple resulting from the process must be accepted, although this must not be obvious. In cast glass and rolled glass, more faults can be expected in the body of the material but obvious blemishes cannot be accepted. In these the external face is easily identified, but in wired glasses there are depressions in the squares or hexagons on the smoother side which could be regarded as faults, except that all sheets are likely to have the same feature.

Thickness of glass varies according to exposure and sound-resistance requirements, but it is quite possible to overlook the fact that, in a tall building, the low windows do not need the same thickness as the topmost, but whether or not the specification writer has appreciated this the inspecting architect can investigate. Rolled or patterned glasses are made in one or two thicknesses in the main, and one often finds that one has specified a pattern which is only available in a thickness quite unsuitable for the large panes to be glazed.

Specialist glaziers work very quickly and, being paid by the job, are likely to press on regardless of other trades, not least puttying on unprimed wood. Despite what has been written in a well-known book on building construction, priming has the purpose of controlling the absorbency of the wood and giving the putty a key, so wood must be primed or the putty will become impoverished. Slovenly back-puttying may be found in the resulting recesses between glass and wood, allowing condensation to collect and rot the wood. Sprigs may be left out or be used in insufficient number—not apparently serious in small squares but their absence always releases the pressure on the back-putty so causing incipient weakness. Sprigs can be seen as front-puttying should not be done until the bed- and back-puttying are firm. Driven sprigs can cause hair-line cracks in the glass which will in time spread right across the pane. Sprigs really must be covered by the front putty or they will rust.

Glazing size in the rebate must be an easy fit to allow putty under the bottom edge in particular, where the weight of the glass may be so great as to squeeze out the putty unless the glass is supported on matchsticks. The other extreme may be found where the glass is only about $\frac{1}{16}$ in/1·5 mm greater than the glass-line—more likely by error than intention—resulting in insufficient putty cover on the glass edge or the front putty having to be built up above the glass line and thus be visible from the interior.

Double-glazing units ought not to need specialist fixing, but those having cemented edges fail so often due to misuse that most makers insist on fixing their own products and will not guarantee them otherwise. The cover of the fixing beads on the channel edge may be greater than the frame design contemplated, the makers apparently being anxious to protect the cementing from exposure to heat, so as the guarantee is affected it is important to see that the conditions of sale, in which this feature may appear, are adhered to. Faults in these units are usually the parting of the cemented edge admitting moisture. One fault experienced and never cleared was an iridescence in some angles of sunlight only. This never appeared at any of the visits of the maker's representative, and the architect saw the effect once only so the makers never had any visual evidence of a defect and refused to replace the very large panel, to the annoyance of the householder.

Where extruded plastics glazing seals are used it is obviously necessary to ensure that the seals match the glass thickness, but where the thickness varies there is scope for error. A late decision to change the thickness of glass may be impracticable because a whole new range of seals, beds and fixing holes would become necessary.

Danger to persons from breaking glass may be noticed in site inspections better than on drawings. Some educational authorities require wired glass to be used in doors, others specify laminated glass, while some object to any glass below waist height, and these principles could well affect other types of build ng. Another danger which may strike one more forcefully on site is the opening window which comes below head-height. Where the public are concerned, this can result in claims for heavy damages for injury. A site decision to raise a footpath can produce just this result. It is not of course the glass which is the danger but the window, a fact discovered too late to change its pattern but which may be reduced at least by fitting some device which limits the opening of the window. If a local authority is sued for damages for injury due to the architect's oversight would the architect be liable?

Glazing in internal doors and partitions is not usually puttied, although there is no sound reason why not, except in polished hardwood which may be stained by the putty. Specifications often still call for the glass to be fitted in chamois leather or felt, ignoring the now common use of self-adhesive black tape which takes care of vibration and reflection from the cut edge formerly specified to be painted matt black.

Ornamental or rolled patterned glass is now available in an ever widening choice, and it is often quite impossible to identify individual types by name, and samples must therefore be available on site. Some are of Continental manufacture so samples are sometimes difficult to come by.

Glass blocks in panels are not intended to take more than self-weight, and this strictly means that the structure should be fully loaded before the panels are built so that deflection of beams may not press on the panels.

Roof glazing on wood astragals is often only bedded on putty, probably because top putty would not last long and would simply trap rain, sprigs sufficing to hold the glass against upward pressure but inevitably rusting. Lead clips are better, dressed down and held by copper nails. As the glass tends to slip it is essential to see that lead, copper or zinc tingles are used, at overlapping ends and at the bottom edge. Today this is an inadequate job when a very good self-adhesive waterproof tape is available which protects the astragal and excludes rain from the long edges of the glass. Patent glazing must be fixed with screws which are non-rusting and preferably non-ferrous, and the bottom clips must also perform the function of glass stops which require the bottom corners of the panes to be cut if the glass is to overhang for draining into a gutter, but this is not necessary in all cases.

Domelights of glass and plastics in the small sizes in some situations provide easy entrance to premises. Some have fixing arrangements that prevent them from being lifted off from outside, but with other patterns it may be necessary to provide additional fixing cleats where site examination shows an easy route to the roof exists for the cat burglar. Another problem with dome lights is the amount of dust that finds its way into the building through the small condensation gap. This is a common experience but cannot be the only one as ventilating kerbs are used in great numbers. Complaints from clients should not come as a surprise.

Plastics for glazing are gaining acceptance increasingly, for windows and doors as well as the established use in roofing. The maker's recommendations should be followed for window and door glazing, but the problem is how to identify which of the apparently identical materials is being used, one being suitable for external use and another largely for internal use as in double glazing. These materials are available in the same thicknesses and are of similar colour, including clear white. As expansion and contraction are much greater than with glass, more clearance in the rebates has to be allowed, but with the difference that, if cut too tightly into the rebate, the material will become concave, but it will not break as glass probably would. It is probably also better to expect it to bend in hot weather than risk it shrinking so much in large sheets that in cold weather the panel could come free of the frame. As cutting can be done by saw and the material can be supplied in large sheets for cutting up on site, the temptation will be to do this by handsaw. The risk here is that a small notch in an edge can in time spread into the panel. The edges must be smoothed before fixing: this is a laborious task which tends to be evaded. Because of the thermal movement fixing in beads is desirable using a non-hardening mastic for bedding and not putty. Problems could arise in glazing in extruded glazing seals because of this movement.

With acrylic roofing sheets thermal expansion and contraction must also be allowed for, so the fixing screws must not be fully tightened, while in long lengths seam-bolting can be necessary. Non-drip quality and non-flam character are usually necessary but are impossible to identify except by burning an edge. Colour change is to be expected to some degree, clear white turning slightly yellow but 'clear white' is a tone which differs among manufacturers so mixing of makes should be resisted.

# CHAPTER 12

# *Heating and Ventilating*

The boundary between what a site architect should know about heating and ventilating and what calls for specialist knowledge is vague, and is not made any clearer by natural bent of the architect. Some architects have found this subject so fascinating that they have made it their main professional interest, not shirking large installations like hotels, historic mansions and schools or colleges. The thought probably appals the academic architect, but for the average type the subject is not so technically forbidding as it seems at first sight, and in managing any large commercial contract he must acquire more than a nodding acquaintance with much technical theory and practice to do his work and exercise the judgement expected of him by heating contractors rather more than heating consultants.

To say that an architect should be able to design an effective installation for domestic hot water and central heating for a house could be true, of a very simple system, which could be entirely satisfactory to the owner but might make a specialist smile indulgently. The principles seem clear, but there are several points according to the system to be adopted which should not be confused. The more sophisticated the installations the more they reach the limits of the architect's experience and knowledge, and so in inspecting these he may have to feel his way. At the moment there appears to be much confusion among architects with mini-bore, micro-bore and small-bore central hot water heating systems, single-circuit, multiple circuit, pumped and gravity systems and where they ought to and need not be used.

Air conditioning however is at the moment expert's stuff, although the principles of the several ways it can be used are clear. Where no consultants are appointed it falls to the architect in office and on site to be satisfied that consistent correct principles are being applied. Even the experts can slip, as happened in an important mammoth job where the 'packaged' boilers were the cause of a storm between maker and installer, because 'de-mineralised' water was not used to fill the system for testing, though the installers knew this was necessary for the system when commissioned.

Heat pumps, solar accumulators, underfloor, overhead and unit off-peak, mass heat accumulators, radiant wall and ceiling infra-red and panel heaters—these are many methods which all need to be understood and nowhere confused in detail.

The side effects of the heating system adopted must also be understood. Those that do not include ventilation can cause high humidity in crowded rooms, with serious effects from condensation in the structure and insulation materials, but this can be easily avoided if the architect knows the danger. It is doubtful, however, whether an architect could be expected to know that a high-velocity air-conditioning system could produce irritating draughts and whistling, or that infra-red ceiling heating may lead to complaints of cold feet from desk-bound staff.

As heating is so closely connected with thermal insulation and economics, there is scope for error in many directions during construction of the building. The main enemy of heating is adventitious ventilation additional to planned air changes, and so poorly fitted doors and windows can spoil a well-designed system, while absence or even perforation of a vapour barrier can lead to water saturation of cellular thermal insulation, making it valueless. The positions of room thermostats affect their effectiveness, for they cannot be reliable if placed in a current of air, warm or cold, rising, dropping or drifting. Thermostats within reach of staff ought to be tamper-proof.

Hot water central heating systems, whether by radiator or convector, must have the radiators balanced on commissioning; this is usually done before the building is occupied so it is bound to be wrong to some extent. One very large public corporation with thousands of buildings is apparently abandoning balancing in practice, for both valves on their radiators are to have wheel heads, enabling staff to adjust the output of each from nil to maximum. The only safeguard to the building manager is the stopvalve controlling the circuit in each of the large rooms, the risk being that if all radiators were turned on fully without regard to a 70°F maximum, the boiler would be unable to cope with the demand, despite the generous surplus that designers generally allow. This is a policy decision taken at a high level and the architects concerned with these buildings have no say whatever.

This is a policy unlikely to be followed generally, so the site architect and the visiting architect must check that balancing is being done before releasing the subcontractors. Balancing is most necessary with gravity hot water systems if radiator sizing has not been strictly suited to demand, the first radiators in the circuit otherwise robbing the later radiators of most of the hot water, a circumstance less probable with a pumped system as distinct from a 'pump-assisted' system.

An architect leaving the design of a heating system by hot water radiators to the builder is often leaving it to the builder's plumber. Where this happens, it is likely that the plumber has done so many installations that he knows where he has gone wrong before and will therefore know what errors to avoid, but this is rash on the architect's part. He should certainly discuss the proposals in great detail, preferably knowing more about the principles than the plumber who may rely on a pump to overcome all difficulties. This it can probably do but it does not make a well-designed system. There are many houses in which a gravity system would work perfectly well, the pump assisting only and overcoming the greater friction of small-bore pipes compared with the old-fashioned 1, $1\frac{1}{2}$ and 2 in/25, 38 and 50 mm pipes—sizes which nevertheless are desirable to and from the boiler without pump assistance on the primary circuit. There is a tendency to think of one circuit per floor, where two circuits per floor would reduce pipework and reduce the vital temperature drop at the return to the boiler, and also ignoring the principle that the maximum horizontal run should be half the vertical rise—which is not a rigid rule by any means. In fact, after much struggling with sagging pipes put in by one of the dimmer plumbers, a small-bore system was made to work satisfactorily where the horizontal run was twice the vertical rise and without the pump which the plumber was so anxious to fit, on a flow temperature of only 150°F too. Possibly the oddest story is of the hotel which replaced the old boiler and gravity system with a pumped system designed on generous lines but found the boiler inadequate. This was replaced by a larger model still, which was also unsatisfactory, while the fuel bill was taking all the profits. The solution was found by a consultant examining every piece of pipe, who discovered a new connection to an old pipe whose other end had been cut and was discharging $\frac{1}{2}$ in/12 mm bore hot water into the garden continuously.

Among the more mundane faults however is that strange neglect of plumbers to avoid air-locks. On two occasions in houses with gravity heating systems the plumbers have taken the flow from the expansion pipe and set it to rise instead of fall with the idea of giving the water 'a good start', instead of which it was of course air-locked. One of the plumbers wanted to fit an air-vent at the high point, forgetting that it would have to be vented every time the flow temperature dropped and was raised again.

Venting of radiators can sometimes be avoided manually if the flow pipe drops to the tops of the radiators, but this is an unusual arrangement not worth pursuing for this small benefit. Pumped circulations do not suffer from air-locks in the pipework but do in the radiators where the pipes have the radiators connected by stubs. In commercial installations the venting may be too great a problem to be solved manually when automatic air-vents are adopted, waste pipes taking any leaking water to safe discharge points, and there must be cases in domestic schemes where they can with advantage be fitted. There is however, a maintenance-free breathing plug which is self-venting.

One characteristic feature of gravity heating systems is that all horizontal runs should be laid to fall in the direction of the return, so all radiators lean a bit to one side—or should in principle—but appearance may demand that they be fixed vertically.

Speaking of fixing, cast iron radiators can have feet or be held on brackets, normally two per radiator, and these really must support each radiator; while pipework in steel will give a lot of support it is not designed to do this, having only pipeclips to hold it in place. Pressed steel radiators have a variety of fixing devices, all of much lighter calibre which must be seen to be firmly fixed. Some have top clips which are adjustable, which in effect leads to carelessness in locating the anchors resulting in the clips not holding the radiator tops firmly.

An occasional fault seen in connections to radiators and in circuit connections is swept tees put in the wrong way round. This has even been seen in a display at the International Building Exhibition. The effect of this is obviously serious on the flow.

All pipework is tested with water on completion, but the real test is after commissioning when expansion should show up leaks.

By this time much pipework is concealed and this practice is not satisfactory, so the architect should test the system with compressed air at a pressure at least twice that of the head of water, and see that the pressure is maintained for 24 hours, though this may not be convenient in practice.

Boiler installations should not require much supervision, though the operation of wallflame and pressure-jet oil burners must be seen to be normal and the time-switches and thermostats to be operative, though their precision may not be determinable except in use. Boilers are equipped with drain points, but where the return pipe rises to the boiler return connection a drain cock should be fitted at the lowest level of pipe.

All pipework should have cut ends reamered, a point frequently ignored in copper installations despite the considerable flange formed on the pipe by the cutters—much the same effect occurs in cutting steel tube. Capillary joints in copper and stainless steel tube should not have more than a thin rim of solder showing, but many plumbers (and heating engineers) like to feed additional solder into the joints, probably because they have had so many failures through omitting thoroughly to clean the grease off the tubes and fittings. In steel pipework an excessive amount of tow or hemp often disfigures joints, particularly those clumsy looking but unavoidable back-joints, and no amount of painting covers up the tow. Steel pipework tends to look uncouth in comparison with copper pipework, but a well-laid out steel job can be a credit to the fitters.

Warm air heating systems having ducts running in all directions in a house must be seen to be left clean and to be capable of being cleaned periodically by vacuum hose. Subfloor ducts in concrete must be damp-proof, either by using waterproof material or by lining concrete ducts with a waterproof membrane, but there is always some doubt because the effective sealing of joints can seldom be seen. The best arrangement is probably that which uses thermal insulating slabs in box form as formers in concrete, all joints being seen to be taped. Directional flow grilles should be checked to ensure that the louvres are locked after setting while fire-dampers have to be checked too, it being presumed that balancing flaps are correctly set by the installers, which is difficult to check. It is as well to see that such a system using a proportion of fresh air does not draw in the exhaust from the fish fryer next door, the sort of revelation which occurs on site only.

Flues from heating plant and incinerators have to be approved by the local Public Health officer so any change in capacity or near outlet which could cause turbulence, such as an additional housing on a flat roof, has to be approved and may be in conflict with architectural sensitivity.

# CHAPTER 13

# *Services*

It is paradoxical that the more elaborate the design of a service the less an architect needs to know, because the installation may be such as to require design by professional consultants or the nominated subcontractors are themselves of a standard of competence and integrity as to be fully capable of designing and executing the installation without the architect's supervision. This does not absolve the architect from responsibility for the installation, and it still leaves him with the responsibility for ensuring that not only one service but all services can be installed without their coming into conflict, such as the discovery on site that a sprinkler main must apparently pass through a ventilating duct for which there is no other route.

An electrical installation on a small job which is the subject of competitive tender usually means that the successful tenderer has cut his profit margins so looks for saving on the job while in progress. When the Supply Companies check the installation before connecting the main supply the architect feels reassured when no fault is detected but this does not mean no fault exists. A wireman may have found that he has not quite enough wire on a reel to complete a run but rather than scrap the length or fit a junction box to enable a good permanent extension to be made he may joint the new extension by twisting the wires together and covering them with insulating tape. All these may be adequately spaced no doubt and electrically continuous at that time, but later on the poor contacts and oxidisation result in poor readings on the Megger and ultimately risk of fire, but at the time of testing there is probably no hint of this. Some architects largely concerned with housing work always check the electrical installation, but where it is accepted that qualified wiremen are employed who abide strictly by IEE Regulations, this is unusual.

Nevertheless the architect could reasonably ask the electricians to show him test readings, but this is only one aspect in that it is virtually impossible for an architect not specialising in electrical work to be aware of the minutiae of the Regulations as a wireman should be, such as the ban on 13 A socket outlets in bathrooms but acceptance of this quite close to sink units, though the practice of earthing metal sink units is probably well known. Also well known no doubt is the unreliability of main water supply pipe as an earth in view of the growing use of plastics pipes for water main supply. Another influence on electrical installations is the attitude of Health Officers to surface wiring in kitchens in catering establishments which the architect may not be aware of until too late to save wasted expense. From time to time changes in attitude form which only the most avid reader of technical papers could know about.

As to gas installations, the practice has been to run the pipework, turn on the gas and check all joints by smell—a quite ridiculously primitive and inefficient means of satisfying the inspector. Now it is common to require air pressure tests, but these should be maintained over a long period, since minute leaks—including defective pipes—do not have much effect over a short period. Reference has been made in Chapter 8 to the dangerous notching of joists, but another factor taking prominence is the avoidance of all possible gas pockets, following two explosions which have been widely reported in the national press. The same principles should certainly be applied to pipework after the meter as before the meter, which imply that no gas pipes should be run in the thickness of a wood joist floor and that casings should be open-ended. Complete separation of electrical and gas installations, at least at meter positions, is called for, but the effectiveness of the separation is often purely nominal.

Thermal insulation installations are regarded as well within the capabilities of most architects, the calculations being fairly simple but the side issues may be considerable. Of these, air-borne moisture is possibly the most insidious, ruining the effectiveness in a short time. In one case, fireproofed wood fibre insulation boards under the sloping asbestos cement sheeted roof became so saturated by process steam the client had failed to tell the architect about that the panels fell out of the channels. In another the condensate in roofing woodwool deck over a coffee bar dripped on the customers and at the same time, through combining with the lime of the screed, degraded the roofing felt, causing drops of black solution to be deposited on the floor. The latter case is one the architect should have foreseen in principle. It is not only moisture, however, which can cause trouble. There was the case of the computer centre where the architect was required to provide insulation to the input ventilation ducts. The material he selected was a firm board, but in time the surface softened and resulted in a flocculent dust being sent into the computer room.

Sprinkler systems are designed around the Fire Offices Committee regulations which pay no attention to architectural niceties, and architects are not well placed to have them varied by relaxation but improvement would probably not cause comment. Approval of a sprinkler layout would normally be an office task, to be considered together with a ceiling layout plan which would take account of angle of cut-off created by beams, which could result in the heads being closer to each other than the regulations require, resulting in greater cost of installation. On site the reasons for locating the heads precisely where shown must be understood, which really leaves the site architect with little scope for deviation. Added to this is the need to ensure that all the pipes can be drained which, with the confusion created by other services and ceiling suspension systems, can be time consuming and extremely difficult in solution.

Virtually all other services being set out on specialists' drawings, the checking of these and co-ordination with other services ought not to be site work, nor the checking that the specialists have correctly interpreted the structural drawings, assuming that all changes the architect has authorised to be made to the structure have been notified in time to the specialists. Fortunately some services are to some extent adaptable to site conditions, such as the runs of small diameter pipes and cables, but not large diameter cables, the minimum radius of bend often creating problems on site which are not realised in the office.

There is also the matter of divided responsibility. A lightning conductor installation required tapes to be run round the parapets of a tall building, these being welded to stubs which the specialists required to be welded to the reinforcement of the structural frame of the building to provide effective earthing. The specialists would not do the welding of the 40-odd stubs because they had no suitable plant or labour, and the main contractors would not do the welding because they could not guarantee the earth continuity required by the conductor specialists. The solution was to finish the reinforced concrete work after which the conductor specialists at considerable extra cost sent labour to the site to cut out concrete to expose reinforcement where required and their own appointed specialist welders made the stub connections, the main contractor then making good to the reinforced concrete. Another main contractor or agent might have made no objection to doing the welding, for which payment would have been made, and earth tests applied before concreting was continued.

Lift wells cause some anxiety in that they seem always to be designed to minima, no allowance for bad building being made, yet we know that dimensional accuracy is seldom better than $\pm\frac{1}{4}$ in/ 6 mm. If a beam casing projects into the well too far it must be cut back to satisfy the lift engineer but must not be cut back if the concrete cover to steel is to be maintained.

Where consultants are instructed they will normally check all installations under their control and certify satisfaction on completion. If they are appointed by the architect with the approval of the client and are instructed to work with the architect, it is reasonable that the architect should receive a copy of the certificate. If the consultants are appointed by the clients and only work along with the architect but not under his control, they may not give the architect copies of certificates even though the works have been done under subcontracts. The client is entitled to know that all the works have satisfied the professional consultants and it is equally necessary that the architect shall have on his file some indication that works done in the building not under his control are acceptable to the client so he may be in the embarrassing position of having to ask the client for copies of the directly nominated consultants' certificates.

Where specialist services have been designed and executed by specialist subcontractors, it becomes necessary for the architect to attend acceptance meetings with these to satisfy himself as far as he can that they function correctly. He could be badly let down, as happened when a large extraction fan failed to perform the duty for which it was designed, its efficiency being only about 75 per cent. This was enough to show that it worked, but only meter tests, applied after complaints some weeks after the architect's acceptance, brought the fault to light. In simple cases fan efficiency can be tested, as in spray booths, by using smoke cartridges, measuring the time taken to clear the atmosphere.

Failure to satisfy design requirements can obviously be serious, possibly preventing an otherwise finished building from being put to use, but some equipment cannot be proved until the building is otherwise finished, as in the case of fans, replacement of which may take months. The installers may present a printed certificate for the architect to sign but if the work has been done under the main contract the main contractor's representative should sign, though he may reasonably argue that he will not sign unless the architect also does so, as the architect is responsible for approving the scheme and its installation. There is no need at all for the architect to sign any certificate, for the purpose of the subcontract is to get the installation required for the building, so it is the duty of the installers to comply. The boot is rather on the other foot, for the architect could require the installers to certify that their design and installation is complete and working to the design standards required before he releases the final payment on certificate. There may also be a number of guarantees issued by manufacturers held by the installers which ought rightly to be passed on to the client. In every case where a service has been provided, it is theoretically necessary that the client should be made familiar with its working, but this is only applied where the service requires unusual knowledge. Cold water and drainage are not so unusual as to require instruction, but functioning of submersible pumps in well bores and sewage plants are outside the normal, and the client must be made familiar with them and how they work.

Every service ought to be fully described in a client's manual, as has been recommended many times, but this is rarely done. The architect keeps in his file the drawings and specifications for all services, whether prepared by his office or by the specialists, and at the end of a contract it would be better to give the client all these documents for his reference if the need arises instead of stowing them away in the architect's dead storage. Preparation of a client's manual requires much thought and involves considerable expense to the architect for which he is not reimbursed beyond the winning of approbation of the client: passing on to him all services documents in a compact easily referrable packet achieves much the same object.

# CHAPTER 14

# *Plasterer*

The client expects a well-finished building whatever price he is paying for it, and the architect is always hopeful that this is what he and the client will get, but the architect knows—and the client may also be well aware—that no one is likely to be entirely satisfied. One does not expect structural failures, but structural shrinkage can scarcely be prevented as moisture dries out, although good design limits its effects as far as possible, but perhaps not far enough to avoid defects showing in plastering. This however one can explain to a client and produce evidence that the architect is not the ineffective ignoramus shrinkage cracks suggest to the client he must be. Shrinkage of lightweight concrete blockwork and sandlime bricks does happen despite all the precautions the architect may have remembered to specify, but there is a limit to the protection from rain which the builder can take to avoid delayed shrinkage. The plasterer then has to make good cracks caused by circumstances outside his control, apart from those he could have prevented if he had not been in so much of a hurry in the first place.

It is well understood but rarely acknowledged that one gets the quality of work one pays for. Local authority housing can seldom be built at the costs allowed by the department, but a builder anxious for work will take on contracts he knows will not pay him the profit he would like, but to get the contract he has to appoint specialist trades quoting the lowest rates without any equation as to quality of work. He is not so silly as to appoint knowingly a specialist tradesman whose work has previously cost him a lot of annoyance, but then he does not always know the specialists. At the same time he is also in the hands of the satisfactory specialist who has run out of labour and has to find new, and therefore untried, men. These he will try out, the labour agreeing, on small jobs, compensating the labour if the work is passable by paying a handsome bonus. If he has no small trial jobs he must take a chance and put his new labour on bigger work. He may find out rather late in the day that the standard is lower than he had hoped for, but not so bad that he can avoid paying the labour nor wasting the material used, and he may resort to hacking it off and replastering by a more reliable work force.

The quality of much of the plastering rests with the travelling foreman as it does in many other trades. He sees the job started and examines quality of work for a few visits, then assumes that all is well, with the result that there is a falling-off in work standards. Architects can suffer from the same failing in their supervision as in their own offices.

As so often the lowest tender must be accepted, whether for a building as a whole or for specialist trades, the quality of work and maybe materials is likely to be reflected. Plastering in particular is a trade into which many infiltrate without years of training. A bricklayer who finds he has the knack of rendering a patch of brickwork decides that he might as well go for the big money calling himself a plasterer, knowing from working on sites for a year or so what materials are used and some of the tricks of using them. As he cannot be charged with the cost of bad work he can float around the building industry leaving a trail of dissatisfied employers and probably architects too.

But apart from the rogue plasterers there are the gangs which must do the job with the utmost speed if their costs and profits are not to be lost, and speed is the enemy of good work. The desirable preliminaries to good wall finish can be ignored at some small cost in time. Given the right rate they can do excellent work if they have not lost their touch. It takes time to plumb and line a wall and dub out the low areas, which is necessary for first class work, but if the rates are low the plasterer will assess the quality of the wall, decide which are the high spots on which the minimum thickness can be applied, then work from there over the rest of the wall giving it the correct thickness. The result is an uneven wall surface as the plasterer knows quite well, but does the builder know and has the architect sufficient perspicacity to find out? A builder working to a low cost may not take a plasterer to task, for remedial work will cost him money so it is better to leave the question to the architect to discover. There is one snag to this: a badly plastered wall may not be obvious until after it has been decorated with emulsion: if the architect condemns the plaster at that stage can he require the builder to remedy it, when it means that the decoration too has to be destroyed? It would appear that as the architect did not tell the builder not to decorate he implicitly approved the plaster.

The faults in plaster finish are usually quite obvious but this depends on the quality of lighting, and it may be this which is to blame for the poor work, for if the plasterer cannot see well he is unlikely to get good results. And if the lighting was poor, did he fail to ask the builder to provide it in time or did he not bother because he knew he would be off on to another contract before the architect realised he ought to condemn it? For once a plasterer goes off a site which involves only a small house it is very difficult to get him back. The problem is not the same at all with the large contract where established plastering contractors are concerned for they must retain the goodwill of the builders and preferably also the architects, and the problem then rests with the plastering contractors as to how they persuade their employee to make good bad work.

The telltales in plastering are the junction lines of wall to wall, wall to ceiling and wall to floor where they ought to be straight without wandering. A well set out wall would have plumbed screeds intermediately in the length and these would have been lined up horizontally so that there would be no waver from the straight line at any angle nor any hollows between screeds, so these are the obvious areas where bad work can be seen.

Faults on walls can be the hollows as remarked above, small areas where the setting coat has not been trowelled smooth, flecks of setting coat fallen from the float and also the float lines seen as arcs which the plasterer has not floated off. These are some of the visible faults, but much can be learned without looking just by running the hand over the wall surface, feeling the undulations which the eye cannot see. Rippling of the surface is often so small that it can only be felt, so it may be acceptable if no strong light falls on it. There are also the junctions with door frames or linings and window frames, where irregularities are obvious to all, but the architraves are expected to cover up the first of these. This the carpenter often cannot do because the setting coat is not finished flush with the wood. Junctions where one day's work meets another, or where one 'lift' is met by another in the height of a wall, are often badly done, resulting in a raised irregular roughly horizontal line.

The last item raises the question as to what should be done. It is a fault with all quick-setting plasters that joining new to old can seldom be done invisibly. The fault referred to is one which cannot be seen by day but can scarcely be ignored by artificial light from above; by daylight the light direction is very similar to that of the fault but at night a shadow is cast. If any plastering is condemned it is usually only a small area requiring patching; this results in the creation of new joint lines of new to old where the new plaster is inevitably either thinner or thicker than the old, resulting in a large new fault where previously there was a small one. If the raised horizontal line is cut out for replastering, after the patch is made there are two horizontal joint lines to complain about above and below the former bad joint. It may be better to ask the builder to see what he can do about the original complaint rather than to condemn the work and specify the action to be taken: it may be that the plasterer can soak the original setting coat, breaking it down so that he can rub down the offending line and scrape off the surplus plaster, but this does the plaster no good at all for it may become quite soft or friable. So long as there is no sign that it is going to fall off this may not matter. The same sort of approach may enable other reparations to be made which specific action detailed in an order would prevent: it would be sufficient to require the builder to make good the defective work without saying how.

There must of course be the borderline cases where poor work is being done although a good price is being paid, as the architect should know without any doubt if bills of quantities have been prepared, though if the contract was a lump sum one he would then base the reasoning more on principle than rates.

It is not only on walls where defects occur. When ceilings were plastered on wood laths the plasterer had to work hard to push the mortar through the gaps sufficiently to turn over to form a key. When metal lathing came into use much of the hard work was removed so there is reduced risk of poor key on such ceilings supported by metal framing, but, given the opportunity, the architect ought to see that key is being obtained together with the use of correct 'metal-lathing plaster' for any other is likely to cause corrosion.

Most ceilings for houses being plastered on plasterboard lath, that risk is eliminated, but there is then the possibility that the wrong kind of skim or setting coat may be used. For one ceiling a plasterer was supplied with a quick-setting plaster for wall finish, but he was not in the least perturbed—in fact he preferred it; his practice was to knock up the plaster and let it nearly go off, then he knocked it up again, thereby killing much of its set. This was the state he liked it to be in and the ceiling he finished was entirely satisfactory for many years. There are no doubt practices in all trades which an architect would frown on because they are not in the book, but if they work and no one suffers there is no reason why they should not be allowed. The snag is that if the architect allows unorthodox practice which results in failure he then has to take the blame, unless he has had the foresight to put the blame on the builder.

One would expect that the plasterer, having being presented with a reasonably flat ceiling surface, would have no difficulty at all in finishing his wet plaster to a good flat surface. One has only to look at the junctions of ceilings with walls to see how far fact is removed from expectation. Undulations can sometimes be seen at the walls, although they are generally to be expected over the ceiling surface but they may not be obvious until a light is shone across it.

Plastering on soffits of concrete slabs cast on metal or other non-absorbent shuttering often suffers from the absence of both mechanical key and suction. This used to be a real problem and it still is to the extent that when the specification was written no problem was expected so no item was taken for overcoming it. Attempts to hack for key were usually ineffective apart from the difficulty of persuading anyone to do such an arduous job well or in fact at all. Fortunately present day bonding compounds have overcome this, but the builder may ask to be compensated for the cost of supplying and applying the bonding coat not included in the specification: this could arouse arguments. If the builder knew the shuttering was non-absorbent then he should have priced the plastering to include bonding coat. If the builder was not required to use a non-absorbent shuttering then it is his own fault that bond is poor, since he probably only used non-absorbent shuttering because it saved him money; he knew when he made the selection that he would have to spend on bonding coat. If however the architect required the builder to use non-absorbent shuttering after letting the contract, the builder would have a good argument for being paid; and if the architect wanted non-absorbent shuttering it may have been because he knew the soffit could be plastered in one coat work instead of two so money was saved on the job, this being after the contract was let. Therefore the architect can afford to authorise payment to the builder of the cost of the bonding coat, which would be much less than the cost of the plaster undercoat. The builder might of course get all the money back by claiming that the non-absorbent shuttering could not be re-used so economically for other soffits, so it cost him more than softwood shuttering, but he should have thought of this one earlier and recorded the possibility when accepting the instruction to use non-absorbent material.

Among the claims to be expected is the one for dubbing-out. Where old walls are being plastered this is almost unavoidable, but the builder ought to point this out before work begins or at least after he has done the dubbing-out, for it is impossible to convince the architect later. If the claim is for work on new walls it is probably a case where the bricklayer has relied on the plasterer to make good his bad bricklaying so, as the builder (and architect?) has accepted undulating brickwork, he ought not to be paid for dubbing-out either as to material or labour. On new walls this is an argument the architect should avoid unless he himself, and not the builder, has let the plastering contract, in which case he ought to be able to deduct from the builder the cost of the dubbing-out.

Much the same sort of claim can arise on soffits. Uneven soffits resulting from poor shuttering are the builder's fault so dubbing-out costs are the builder's responsibility. Uneven soffits also occur where precast slab units are used, the unevenness being at its worst where humped prestressed concrete beams are concerned, for they are often incorrectly sorted before placing. This is truly a thorny problem. If the differences in soffit level are apparently small, the architect may take the view that they are not worth bothering about, but if the base coat plaster is a sanded one it is not easy for the plasterer to average out the thickness by giving a thin coat on the low areas and thick coat on the high ones. At a difference of over about 3 mm it is quite likely that dubbing-out may be necessary, but it could also be said that the only extra cost lies in the greater amount of material used and not in labour in a separate operation. There is a limit to this, however, for the weight of the wet plaster may be too great for the suction.

It is also necessary to determine who was responsible for the uneven soffit. Makers of prestressed precast units know very well that humping often develops and that when they contract to place their units they should sort them to minimise the differences in soffit level. They also know that, where infill blocks rest on shoulders between precast units, the levels of these blocks can differ very considerably from the soffits of the units they are resting on, and so they should impress on their fixers the need to maintain levels. Then there are the simple non-prestressed precast concrete units which ought to be flat without exception, but these somehow seldom finish quite flat. Perhaps this could be due to poor bedding on brickwork, but who provided the bedding—the layers or the builder?

There are clearly a number of factors to be taken into account and none in the foregoing appear to entitle the builder to any additional money from the client, nor the makers of the units either, but the architect is unlikely to escape from being called on to agree to a claim, so he automatically finds himself acting as judge.

Architects used to abet the resistance to defects by specifying that all external arrises should have Keene's Cement wings on each side to give strength where abuse in use was most likely to occur, and this was all very well when lime plaster was the general plastering material, but it unfortunately continued into the hard plaster era, and raised junctions are often seen where Keene's Cement wings have been specified. Resistance to damage at angles is still necessary, particularly where trolleys and furniture are moved much, but helpful in the house too. The Victorian staff bead was possibly the best solution which had the added advantage that where an angle was out of plumb this was not made obvious in the wallpapering because it had to be stopped on either side on the staff bead. Current practice is to specify metal angle beads bedded in the first coat and nailed, but the lines these assume need watching, for they must be straight and plumb, yet having very little innate stiffness they can wander in the fixing.

Specifications are often copied, one from another, without much thought as to different conditions likely to arise in uses of buildings. Reinforced arrises may not be needed in a house but they may be highly desirable in offices. Gypsum casings to columns may also be acceptable in housing but may only last a short time in a school, while gypsum plaster in a works corridor traversed by trolleys and men swinging tool kits, or teenagers swinging bulging brief cases in school corridors would be a poor choice, the damage resulting not being prevented by reinforced angles. The architect on site may realise that the specification needs amendment to suit the harsher conditions the new building demands.

Some architects firmly believe in continued use of lime plaster, possibly gauged with Portland Cement, because it is softer and does not cause the same hard echoes which gypsum plaster is said to produce. There are many arguments against lime plaster, one being its softness, another being the long time it requires for drying out and the effect it has on decorations, but these objections can be modified by adding hardening materials like Portland cement to the base coat up to equal parts with lime, and gypsum cement to the setting coat of slaked lime, by which time we are back to a plaster which is harder and more resistant to damage than some gypsum plasters. The makers of gypsum plaster, having produced a semi-solid base coat with inherent softness or at least compressibility, have countered this by evolving a harder base coat, and this may give the architect a solution to an unexpected difficulty. It seems that although plasterers at one time thought nothing about rendering the interiors of buildings in cement and sand mixed 1:4, they now find this or the currently popular mix of 1:1:6 much too laborious, so even when a really hard wall finish is required as in factories there may be considerable difficulty in getting the work done. That it must be done sometimes cannot be denied but it may mean paying rather more than for gypsum plastering.

Another aspect of this is where internal dry lining is adopted where the harsh use of the building may demand that greater thickness of plasterboard ought to be authorised than the architect in his office foresaw. He may also realise that the hollow casings to columns ought not to be in plaster at all but some more forgiving material which is nevertheless more resistant to hammering, or they may be given a solid core. These cost a little more and this may be difficult to justify to the client who expected the architect to be aware of the risks before tender stage.

Substitution is not rife in plastering but quality of material is clearly just as important as in any other trade, with the added risk that gypsum plasters are even more at risk than the Portland cements. Thickness of plasterboard may be wrong in that only 9 mm thickness can be obtained from stock when 12 mm is required for the span but the job must not be held up. Then there is the use of foil-backed plasterboard, which can be used quite pointlessly because the foil makes no contribution to thermal insulation or protection from vapour but it ought to be used where it can contribute, if delivery can be made; if not, what other insulation material can be used and how effective is it in comparison and can the builder really make a claim for extra cost?

External renderings seldom give trouble today when machine-applied coatings are used, but where traditional specifications are followed the old troubles are likely to crop up again. These include cracking of the finish and loss of adhesion. That the traditional specification should be used at all may be an error in that this was generally regarded as 'cement-rich' which is so conducive to shrinkage, whereas today's 1:1:6 mix is less likely to crack—that is if the plasterer does not enthusiastically rub up the surface to bring up the 'fat' (in other words laitance) which in presenting to him a close texture gives him the idea that it must be the more waterproof. The first requisite is of course that the wall shall have good suction, and this is where so many bricks fail and where some stones have too much—as bricks may also.

The architect cannot know how suitable a wall is to receive rendering, and this may alter from day to day according to whether rain falls or not. It could be worth while having a trial area applied both to test the habits of the plasterer and the suction of a dry wall.

There are many varieties of external rendering from single-coat machine-applied facings on raked joints to the coarse applications where each float load is spread but not levelled, and the worry will be whether the approved treatment will be applied consistently throughout, especially where a number of plasterers are employed on one building. In this connection the finishes known as pebble-dashing and those having spar or other uncoated particles thrown on to wet mortar can be the most unsatisfactory. This may be through the plasterer being careless in failing to catch the rendering at the right time when it is neither too wet nor too dry to hold the particles. Unfortunately if there is variation in application it is very difficult to put right; a patch nearly always remains different. This is true where traditional materials are used but where correction must be made it is possible that one of the brush-applied bonding coatings may provide the solution. Equally important of course is certainty that the supply of particles will not run out.

The easiest rendering to correct is that category using clear resin cements where, given that the original materials are still available, there should be no 'tide mark' where a patch meets the original

work. Sometimes these renderings are divided by plastics strip for
a pattern or to limit working area; these strips are quite flimsy
and can be pushed out of position quite easily, but because the
plasterer is so near to the work he may not be aware of this.

Such a fault may not be observable until the scaffolding is down,
and this applies also to all renderings, but it does mean that the
architect should inspect the work at each scaffold level. The gross
irregularity of surface in rough-cast and pebble-dash finishes at
close quarters may shock him but this is not necessarily a fault so
long as the corners have been well controlled. He must see that the
plasterer has conscientiously carried the rendering into all reachable
spaces and up tight to the undersides of window sills and returns
to frames and at soffits. If the plasterers know the architect makes
a habit of looking closely at their work and commenting on it they
are less likely to scamp it. The visiting architect is of course in the
difficulty that all the work may have been done between visits when
he has to rely on his binoculars and perilous leaning out of windows.
It is no excuse that inspection is difficult, but it might be mitigation
to have recorded to the builder that he must insist on an approved
standard of work being maintained, stressing the need to ensure
that proper attention be paid to junctions with frames, sills, etc.,
the 'etc.' covering so many areas which he may not have thought
about.

Where solid walls are rendered from ground up, there is some
controversy as to whether to form a break at the horizontal damp-
proof course level which can look unsightly. Whether there is a
real risk of capillarity drawing moisture from below the DPC into
the upper wall is a question he may have to consider, but it is not
likely to arise where cavity walls are used. Another question may
be whether he wants provision to be made for leakage of water
passing through the external wall at lintel level. There seems to
be no authoritative guidance on this, but if the leakage is so great
it is likely that the rendering is not performing its main function.

There are proprietary finishes and those using exfoliated vermiculite,
acoustic plasters, imitation stone, fibrous plaster and plastic paint
which the inspecting architect must understand, but this is less
necessary where specialists apply their own materials, although he
must always be on the alert for abuses, damage that these specialists
cause to other work and which is caused to theirs; this is a fruitful
area for difficult decisions but an unavoidable one.

Fire protection of structural steelwork by plasterwork in one form or another is a case where the plasterer's complete understanding of the requirements and the methods to be adopted to satisfy them is necessary, if he is to be fairly content that the work is done conscientiously while the visiting architect is away from the site and the builder has other problems to attend to. Failure of metal lathing fixing under fire and omission of wire binding can have such serious results that a charge of negligence against the architect for failure to specify the measures adequately and to supervise the work during progress would in many jobs be difficult to rebut, though the architect would no doubt bring in on his side the builder who might in turn bring in the plastering contractors, while the true cause of the failure, the journeyman plasterer, remained serenely indifferent to the results of his casualness. Really this work ought to be inspected at intervals, such as metal fixing adequacy, binding wire application and fixing of metal beads and final coating, with sample plaster from the batch for examination as to vermiculite or other aggregate mix to gypsum cement. Where asbestos or similar spray protection is adopted, the overall dimensions give the clue to the net thickness of material, which ought to be checked and not left unexamined.

There was a time when wall tiling was a separate trade, but plasterers have to a large extent taken it over except where large areas of tiling are required. The choice will normally lean towards the specialist and this can certainly be justified when looking at some of the results of plasterers' tiling. Introduction of bituminous, rubber and plastics based adhesives largely superseding Plaster of Paris and Portland cement has given rise to the idea that anybody can do wall tiling, and there is no doubt that a good handyman taking an interest in the work can give better results than a second rate plasterer.

When a wall had to be prepared for tiling by a backing of Portland cement and sand, the excellence of this surface affected the quality of the whole tiled wall. Now that thick-bed adhesives can be used the problems are greater for there is no exact datum for the tiler. Not only can individual tiles be off the correct planes horizontally and vertically, but the whole wall surface may undulate.

Tiles are made within fine dimensional limits when made of fine clay, but the tolerance increases as the clay becomes coarser. Tight joints are practical in one but not in the other and a satisfactory joint pattern can only be adopted which acknowledges the dimensional variations in batches of tiles. Variation in joint thickness of a nominal 6 mm would not be noticeable within 0·5 mm, but this would be obvious where tight joints are required. Suppliers of the tiles may recommend a joint thickness, but if not the plasterers may bring the point to the architect's notice; on the other hand some plasterers, told to lay to tight joints tiles that suffer considerable dimensional variation, may endeavour to do just that with the result that some joints are tight and a fair proportion are not, giving a very untidy overall impression.

The overall impression is what the client is likely to get but the architect wants more. Tile courses have to be horizontal, including the individual tiles, and vertical joints too must be accurately plumbed, and all tiling should be quite flat, which the hand by sweeping in an arc over the surface can tell much better than the eye. Where tiling is taken to room height, there is some risk that the tiler will presume that the ceiling is level and work down from this, which can result in all the courses being obviously out of level at window and door head levels, where there is very little chance of masking the error.

The sheets of mosaic tiles can be misleading in that the tiler has his work covered up as he beds the tiles. Being so close to the work he cannot stand back to compare horizontal with horizontal so he ought to use a level as every sheet is fixed; this is more necessary than with the larger tiles which can be set out by rods, provided always that the bases for the rods have been correctly levelled.

Treatment of angles should be agreed with the tiler; one does not expect to have cut tiles on either side of an external angle, but if agreement to this cannot be reached is it possible to satisfy the other convention that internal angles shall have tiles of equal width on either side? Perhaps it is, if tight joints have not been specified and a little 'spreading' of the tiling can be accepted but this would only be possible on long lengths. And if a height above floor was specified, did this take into account the exact size of tile, joint thickness and relationship with window ledge and lintel and door heights? If not, and if it is important that the tiling shall line with these levels, how is it to be done? One expects full tiles at the top and bottom of tiling, and one likes full tiles at ledges, lintels and heads, but usually something has to be sacrificed and the tiler will want to know what; and if cut tiles must be accepted at ledges and lintels should the cut be made so that the rounded edge is retained on the vertical tiles or the horizontal ones? How ragged is the cut edge of that kind of tile and perhaps the ragged edge ought to be on the less obvious plane at the sacrifice of the joint line. A simple trade has a multitude of queries for the architect.

# CHAPTER 15

# *Painting and Decorating*

These well-used terms hide the more serious implications of preservation. While we increasingly use less corrodible or degenerating materials, we are liable sometimes to overlook well established facts; *e.g.* that two well-known non-rusting metals, if placed in contact, are self-destructive while other less antagonistic metals when touching lead to destruction of one of them. We are also apt to assume that a metal with a certain non-paint finish which weathers well in one situation will not be affected by different conditions in another. We also have a metal which lasts well when regularly washed, but is gradually destroyed if not—a point for the client to record but not always easy to ensure attention, especially as no paint treatment is called for.

It is likely that much more paint is used protectively than decoratively, but one often requires the two qualities in the one coating, which in some paints may not be available. Aluminium alloy sheet fastened to mild steel sheeting rails should be separated at least by a coat of paint, but how thick and of what kind? It is really rather vague and if the paint is one that shrinks and cracks its value must be small. Some will say the paint must be bituminous, others that a chlorinated rubber type would be more reliable, some that a zinc-rich primer is best of all. There are the cases too where the backs of mild steel sheets are to be painted with two coats because, once erected, no one can reach those surfaces again. This case is strictly one of bad design or specification for another solution should have been found if at all possible. The paint then must cling well, must not harden due to heat or cold and yet not soften either. One then has to ensure that it is applied to dry surfaces, in two coats moreover. This is really asking too much when there are many waterproof films or membranes available which

155

would do the job better; these can be stuck and can be seen up to the moment of covering over.

The 'paint' may not be one of the traditional variety at all. Although brush, spray or roller application may be suitable, the absence from their composition of resin oils makes the description 'paint compound' more suitable. Maintenance departments with wide experience over generations of all sorts of paint applications often insist on preservation of steel by essentially traditional paints using resin oils, lead in one form or another, colour pigment and driers. Makers of later formulations may scoff at this hide-bound attitude but fail to shake the stubborn loyalty of the traditionalists. But there are certainly changes and improvements in the 'traditional' paints, and much benefit can be gained from the use of anodic and zinc-rich primers, so valuable to touching up areas where a galvanised finish has been damaged, which must be looked for in the site inspections.

Particularly in industrial work aesthetics may have to take second place to preservation, especially when the choice of a light colour results in poorer protection than a darker colour. A head-on collision with the plant manager could result, to the detriment of the architect's *amour propre*. To compromise by covering up the bituminous paint even of light colour with an oil paint would be inviting failure until the base had hardened and was sealed with an aluminium primer or something similar.

Paint technology is becoming ever more complex with changes continuously being made that the average architect can scarcely be expected to know or understand. Once we always specified pink priming for softwood, though some priming was more spirit than pigment, and others could be rubbed off the wood by the hand. The BRS finding that acrylic primers held to the wood appreciably better than traditional primers and were easier to use has had a strong influence. Undercoats and gloss finishes once acclaimed as 'linseed oil' products are commonly superseded by products having constituents we know by name better as plastics. But not all architects and builders are convinced that these are better than gloss paints, which certainly go dull but at least do not split and trap water beneath the gloss film, rotting the wood. The man paying the maintenance costs is the one whom the choice of type of paint must satisfy. In brief, on all large and industrial contracts it is as well for the inspecting architect to agree the painting specification or schedule of decorations with the client and preferably also the nominated manufacturers of the protective materials, whatever may have been taken in the bills. Re-decoration contracts are full of problems, for the previous decorative materials must be identified to ensure compatibility of materials and firmness of hold. To apply emulsion paint to a wall previously treated with distemper would be unwise.

Treatment of corrosion such as rust relies very much on workmanship. One can attack it with a cold chisel, a wire brush, an abrasive cloth or chemicals, including recently developed 'rust converters', and prime again with red lead, zinc chromate or zinc-rich coats. Should they be well brushed out or 'flowed' and how does either affect the appearance of the finish coat, or perhaps brush marks do not matter?

Deposits on aluminium alloy, copper, zinc, etc. need less fierce cleaning, but all these have highly tenacious chemical reactions to exposure and must be treated before decoration will adhere well. Some are best prepared by acid solution and some by abrasion, some not being readily seen to have been done before decoration is applied. These labours give little satisfaction to the journeyman painter; it is all a chore, but there are some conscientious characters among them, although all the work nevertheless requires inspection by the architect.

Existing plastered walls and ceilings may have surfaces apparently good for recoating until rubbing with the hand results in showers of flaking dust. The customary 'rub down' or 'wash down' is then useless for the base must be fixed somehow, perhaps by using a binder coating or lining paper which is only effective where the general mass of the area gives it a good hold. It is a well-established fact that a harder finish cannot be applied to a softer base, in any materials.

Some industrial atmospheres in buildings are inimical to conventional decorative treatments, while some processes are dangerous to health, requiring breathing equipment for the decorators. What a firm's own maintenance painters will put up with, a painting contractor's men will not necessarily agree to do, and it is dangerous for the supervising architect to demand that they carry out the appointed work. A situation like this should not arise where a schedule of works has been prepared by the architect, for he would be expected to have examined the working conditions before issuing it, and to have ascertained from the works manager what protection or precautions the painters would need.

The old practice of requiring succeeding coats of paint of a system to be tinted differently is difficult to enforce now, as colours are brought on site ready mixed. It presents no serious problem really, for a perceptive eye should be able to see whether one or two undercoats have been applied. It is not so easy to say whether one or two finish coats have gone on, a recommendation which some manufacturers of gloss paints make. The addition of stainers to the first of two coats of like materials is quite practicable both on the job and by the appointed paint manufacturers, but it will be met with a good deal of opposition and add to cost. A possible alternative is to insist on the first of two like tints being completed and certified by the architect as complete before the second matching coat is started.

It is of course a fallacy that a second finish coat will mask a badly applied underfinish coat, or any other coat. Coarse brush marks must be rubbed down, not overlaid with another coat of paint. Stippled texture, once customary in good quality contracts, is a refinement to remove all traces of brushwork; it is of doubtful merit today and roller application emulates it satisfactorily.

Brushmarks are of no consequence in purely protective painting while some coatings do not flow out readily. The ordinary decorative paints and emulsion paints need little care when the precept to 'apply with the grain, spread across the grain, finish with the grain' is followed, but each application should be lighter than the previous one. The result on application may first show crossing lines, but these should flow out if the paint is applied at a suitable temperature. On other than wood surfaces the same principles should be followed for gloss paints, but this is not correct for whitewash, distemper and emulsion paint, when application in all directions gives better results. Attempts to get away with only one coat of paint or emulsion are rarely successful on an old hard surface, as differences in tone nearly always show through. The only way it can be done is to apply a well-brushed-out coat followed immediately by a full coat while the first is still tacky, but this involves the risk of the new coating peeling very easily.

Decorating externally early in the day, even in summer, and at various times in other seasons carries with it the risk of surface dampness imperceptible to the eye. Curiously this is not always destructive to keying to the base as though the moisture was displaced by the brush. Clearly this risk should not be taken but how can one stop a painter starting his day normally at 8.30 a.m. if he works in shielded areas such as eaves overhang even if there is a morning mist. An architect resident on site can form an opinion but the visiting architect can only ask questions.

On plaster surfaces various pre-treatments may be suggested by the builder at extra cost. The surface has too much suction or has no suction, it might be as well to defer decoration or apply a coat of sharp colour or Clearcolle or a coat of thinned emulsion and so on. Some of these are more likely on some surfaces than on others. Some gypsum plaster applied to cement and sand base coats will sweat and then develop a great thirst so should have a coat of sharp colour immediately after the plaster is applied which acts as a key and saves time in the end. The lore of the painter is extensive and the inspecting architect is expected to know it and give knowledgeable instructions on it.

Spray painting on wood is sometimes objected to because the paint cannot be impressed into grain as in brush work, and this is a fair view, but on other surfaces there is less objection. The objection to spraying on wood cannot be overcome by using greater air pressure for the paint just bounces off again. On plaster surfaces good spray painting should give just as good a finish as roller application and probably better in the narrow widths where a brush must supplement the roller.

Cutting-in to edges like window frames has to be watched. The putty or bead must be painted fully to seal with paint the junction with the glass to a minimum extent, but some painters carry the paint on to the glass too far, where its adhesion is poor. Clumsiness is also seen in carefully painting around non-ferrous metal. This is an interesting throw-back to the origins of painting to protect and not just to decorate. There does not seem much point in leaving unpainted on the edge of a door the darkly oxidised brass fore-end of a mortice lock or the case of a brass flush bolt, so long as the paint does not stop the ironmongery from operating.

If a particular brand of paint or emulsion has been specified, it may be rewarding to wander into the builder's site store ostensibly to satisfy one's self that it is dry and weather-tight, but also to see whether the materials there are the brands expected, paints and emulsions among others.

In built-up areas, flue emissions can be troublesome at all stages of external decoration. Smoke deposit on painted walls can be removed with normal washing solutions like sugar soap, while the spot stains of fuel oil discharges are more resistant and are liable to appear on each successive coating. There is nothing the builder can do to prevent this happening, while the painter may try to overpaint the spots which then turn into streaks, which are quite obvious in light colours. This is only one of the many small matters that observation may disclose at the inspections.

There was a time when the specification required the painter to apply the paint as delivered in the can without the addition of thinners. This ignored conditions of application. In mild weather and on surfaces which are not cold there was no objection to the clause, but in cold weather working outside a building in a bitter wind it is not only the painter who is affected. Some paints are heavier to apply than others irrespective of whether they are lead or zinc based, because of the nature of the oils used, but all paints with one exception become more viscous as temperature drops. The exception is that kind of paint formulated for use in cold stores.

Today paint manufacturers allow thinners to be used, and this is for two reasons. One is to make the paint sufficiently fluid for the painter to apply it all day long without exhaustion, and the other is to enable him to brush it out which if not done will result in 'curtaining', which often only shows when it is too late to go back to brush it out.

The old specification clause was well intentioned in ensuring that all coats were as full-bodied as the paints allowed and that must still be the aim. Prior to 1939 the thinner was always expected to be best turpentine, but today the term is 'thinners or white spirit' which seems just as satisfactory as expensive turpentine.

What is a full-bodied coat varies with the surface and the kind of paint, but an unnecessarily heavy coat does no one any good. A full-bodied coat of gloss paint will not necessarily be so opaque as to obliterate a base of a different colour as an undercoat made for the purpose will. A full-bodied undercoat will not always obliterate the grain of joinery softwood nor many hardwoods, so it may be difficult to decide whether a paint has been thinned or not. There is no doubt about a paint that requires to be thinned, for its application tends to be uneven and the painters are grumbling. On the other hand the extensibility of gloss paints by thinners is remarkable. On one job in mid-winter a painter was applying gloss coat of middle blue to undercoated doors of a large workshop in a biting north wind on a Saturday morning when the architect was not expected. The painting was progressing well but what drew the architect's attention was the ease with which the painter applied the paint with the grain, across the grain and finished with the grain in one opaque coat. On looking into the paint kettle he saw he could slop the paint about in a way the manufacturers never intended but the painter denied it was thinned. It was his employer who confirmed that it had been thinned, easily proved by the large amount of thinners used and small amount of paint relative to the surface covered. Although wrong in principle the painter was right in practice for he could not have used the paint as supplied. Another thinned coat on top of the first gloss coat gave a very good job but it cost his employer a few pounds more. In this case the paint was thinned too much.

## CEILING AND WALL PAPERING

Cracked plaster should not be papered over without additional work. Lime plaster ceilings are prone to cracking and some detachment from the laths. Even cracks only $\frac{1}{16}$ in/1·5 mm wide in walls show under the paper, the more so if the edges are on different planes. How far the plasterer as distinct from the decorator should become involved must depend on the safety of a ceiling and the quality required in the finished work. Much wall lime plaster is hollow but will stay in position despite cracks, so if there is no bulging indicating imminent break up it is usual to leave it, for once a hollow patch is cut out most of the rest of the wall will become hollow too. Hairline cracks can often be filled by brushing in a hemi-hydrate plaster, but others have to be V-cut and stopped by the painter.

Lining paper can be necessary to make a cracked plaster surface suitable for decorative paper hanging, while heavy papers need this as a base in most cases. One may in ignorance of the condition of wall and ceiling surfaces simply specify that these are to be hung with paper at £x per piece, then find considerable extra cost is involved through cracked surfaces and selection of unexpectedly heavy paper, both requiring lining.

Plasterboard ceilings finished with filler to feather-edge or skim coat often crack at the joints, but this should be so slight as to need little work beyond brushing in emulsion or a similar filler.

Suction in walls and ceilings has to be controlled as excessive suction takes the moisture out of the paste with two effects. In one the paper is difficult to handle because 'slip' is lost, which the paper-hanger will avoid at all costs, but the other effect is seen in badly prepared walls where an untreated area does not hold the paper. The result of this is seen in humid conditions when the unstuck area of paper will blister. This is not easy to detect on inspection but it is likely to occur where a patch of new plaster is made, the old plaster having much less suction than the new.

Edge-to-edge papering is essential in linings as well as decorative papers, the former always being hung at right angles to the decorative paper. In ceilings the lengths of decorative paper should run from the major source of daylight, and in normal work joints should be virtually invisible, but in repetitive patterns, unless all lengths are equally pasted and allowed equal time for absorption, unequal expansion will result, so the pattern gets out of gear on adjacent lengths.

The universal adoption of ready-trimmed edges to wallpaper rolls risks damage to edges which naturally the paperhanger will disguise if possible, but this is worth looking for. Where a roll is so damaged as to be largely unusable, if the builder has not bought in excess to allow for this there is the possibility that replacements in coloured patterns will differ slightly but perceptibly. The replacement roll must be ordered quoting the batch number on the rolls of the original order. This is of course no help at all when the manufacturers are abandoning one season's selection, hence running out of stock. One device used to spin out shortage of paper but only possible with heavily patterned designs is to hang the walls with deliberately short lengths, the bottom ends of which are not cut but torn irregularly. The lowest part is then papered in short lengths in matching offcuts which have their top edges irregularly torn but pasted over the short piece stuck earlier and pattern matched exactly. Given that the bottom patch is torn from the back and that care has been taken, the join is very difficult to see, especially in being well below eye-level; but it may be noticeable in artificial light cast from a high level.

Modern pastes do not stain the surfaces as traditional pastes do, while the objection that their use was not so easy as the old pastes is being overcome as 'slip' is restored in the new pastes. One result is that the paperhanger tends to become somewhat careless in handling both paste and paper. Today's pastes do not stain, so in general any on the face of the paper is not seen, but on some papers the paste softens the colour print causing smudging. To avoid this the tendency is to reduce pasting at the edges which in turn can result in the edges not being well stuck. In a humid atmosphere the edges may lift and will not go back when a drier climate returns. Embossed papers need particular care in hanging to ensure that the pattern is not flattened, especially when the roller is used at the edges.

Very long 'drops', as on some stairs walls, put a lot of strain on newly pasted pieces, which as a result may tear before they can be placed on the wall. Two paperhangers working together can share the weight to some extent, but the wet strength of the paper should be borne in mind when making a selection in trying situations.

In old premises, and to a lesser extent in more recent buildings, the angles of walls are by no means plumb. It is then impracticable to bring one piece of paper round the corner, whether an external or internal one, for inevitably on one face or the other the pattern will emphasise the fault, especially when a pattern with a strong stripe is chosen. The paper must be cut to the angles with only a small turn round each corner to hold the pieces one to the other. Undoubtedly the angles will be seen to be leaning or hollow but this is a better course than trying to bring the pattern round; a paperhanger may nevertheless ask for instructions as to how the architect wants the problem treated.

Electrical roses and switchplates in new work can usually be removed, provided the current has not been switched on, and only then can a good job be done. In other circumstances, where the current cannot be switched off, the paperhanger must cut around the roses and plates, though he may undo some screws to lift them a little off the wall to push the paper behind, but this is risky. One must expect the cutting to be a little crude then but the architect will have to make up his own mind as to what is acceptable. The same sort of problem arises and on a larger scale where heating radiators are concerned. They cannot be turned off and removed in the middle of winter and it is equally impossible to hang wallpaper behind them. The solution if any is one that the architect must search for with the client, which might be to paper only as far behind each radiator as 3 in/75 mm or thereabouts from sides and top.

Staining of walls above radiators by ionisation of dust particles cannot be stopped, except perhaps by surface thermal insulation. If the wallpaper is washable periodic cleaning is possible, but the alternative may be the application to the wallpaper of one of the clear and invisible brush coatings. The trouble with these is that it is almost impossible to detect which walls have been treated. There is in fact a slight darkening of the paper so a complete wall surface has to be treated, but this is too slight for the inspecting architect to satisfy himself that the work has been done, but he can ask to see the empty containers if he doubts the builder's word.

Where to start wallpapering a room may matter considerably if a well-defined large scale pattern is used. If there is a chimney breast with central fire opening the main pattern feature will usually be centred on the breast, the paperhanger then working away from the centre in both directions which may result in chaos where the two directions meet so further planning is necessary to find more subtle adjustments to the pattern rhythm, as at corners, windows and doors. An experienced paperhanger will have forseen all this before starting work but the inspecting architect should find out his intentions. Sometimes it is better not to have a central panel but centre joint instead so that more of the main pattern may be seen at the edges of the flank than would be the case with a central panel.

# CHAPTER 16

# *Roads and Pavings*

Design of roads to be taken over by the highway authority must be to standards acceptable to it, but on private land the only control is what will work and remain serviceable. The highway authority's specifications are often considered extravagant, but they are concerned to avoid expensive maintenance arising out of future loadings quite as much as using a good factor of safety. Minimum crossfalls, maximum sizes of concrete bay, maximum distances between gullies, etc. as laid down by the authority are good guides for the design of private roads, but a private road carrying only private cars can be of much lighter construction than a public highway on a housing estate. This can be misleading, for the very existence of a road for vehicles can be a welcome solution to an access problem for a very heavy lorry carrying a very heavy piece of machinery, to the destruction of the lightweight road.

The base for the road is even more important than the specification of the wearing surface, for drainage must be good for stability and avoidance of frost heave. Soft spots are just as important for elimination as under buildings, and the hardcore must be at least as good as under floors, for the latter may be kept dry while the former is damp for a large part of its life, and so must not break down through dampness or frost. Angularity which locks the pieces together is more important than under floors where the hardcore cannot spread, being contained to some extent by walls, and the elimination of unacceptable matter like old plaster, old wood, loam, clay, rags and tree stumps that are frequently present is essential. Rolling must be continued until it has no effect on the hardcore, but if breaking up begins then either the roller is too heavy or the quality of hardcore is poor. When this is blinded the gradients can be checked.

Where kerbs are specified (and they perform a function only where

165

the carpet may spread) they are useful as formers for concrete road-ways, but this requires that the kerbs follow exactly the gradients of the road, which may look more than a little odd.

Preservation of hydration water in a concrete mix requires a waterproof layer under the carpet, and mesh reinforcement 1 in/ 25 mm from the bottom surface requires spacers, but they are very seldom seen, the rough-and-ready custom being to spread a thin layer of concrete on the mesh then lift it up with some sort of hook to let the concrete spread under it then carry on concreting—this is slovenly but it works. Some more fastidious people require 1 in/25 mm diameter rods to be laid under the mesh while the full depth of concrete is laid, on the presumption that it will flow under the mesh, the rods then being pulled along the base in readiness for the next concreting stage. This is difficult to do where there are end stops for the bays as well as kerbs. Road makers like to finish the edges of the bays with a wood float, smoothing the tamping marks, but this does no real good except that it is possible to put a slight round on the arrises against the end stops or expansion jointing material. The old practice of curing by covering with straw and tarpaulins has been abandoned in favour of the much more effective but not so clearly seen one of a sprayed-on plastics coating keeping evaporation down and frost out to a large extent by containing the warmth developed in hardening.

Bitumen-type carpets harden with the evaporation of the fluxes while the asphalt-type harden by the cooling of the asphalt, both types being well covered by British Standards. The former can be kept for weeks but the latter is only useful within a limited range of temperatures.

Road carpeting ought to be specialist's work, but builders often do patch repairs with various degrees of success, and having done some work of this nature may be tempted to take on bigger work, but this is not to be encouraged. The accuracy in laying and rolling the base coat of a two-course specification is most important, for inaccuracies cannot be corrected effectively in rolling the wearing coat. Puddles should not be allowed where normal crossfalls are intended, but there are inevitably small depressions whose depth should not exceed the thickness of a two-penny piece. Corrections can be made easily in cold bitumen carpeting, but in asphalt carpets the material in which a depression is found will have lost its essential warmth, so a patch can only be made by cutting out a square and filling with fresh hot asphalt. Manholes cannot be set until the road is otherwise complete, when they can be bedded to level and filled around with road material.

Footpath pavings in cold bitumen must be contained by kerbs, which can finish flush to enable rain to run off. The open texture of the carpet is usually blinded with fine material rolled in, but a weakness of this type of paving is that, unless it is well used, grass and other weeds soon get a grip. Both roads and footpaths improve in use by closing the pores of the material.

Paving slabs require less crossfall for drainage, are longer lasting and cost a good deal more than cold bitumen paving. Some specifications require paving slabs to be laid on 3 in/75 mm concrete, but this is not usually necessary. A good specification calls for 3 in/75 mm of clinker followed by the bedded slabs, but even this leaves some vegetable soil under the path. As clinker is scarce, all-in ballast is usually substituted, which is well rolled, to receive a stone-lime and sand bed for the slabs, this being more amenable to flow under the slab than a Portland cement and sand bed. Badly consolidated bases come to light equally under tar paving and slab paving but the former shows up even the small defects which the paving slabs can bridge. Slabs are often closely butted making pointing impossible while allowing grass to grow. Spacing at about $\frac{1}{4}$ in/6 mm allows the joints to be pointed in cement and fine sand.

Internal paving in cement and sand or 'granolithic' is recomended to have a minimum thickness of $1\frac{1}{2}$–2 in/38–50 mm, but some paving specialists are ready to guarantee no cracking and good adhesion to a concrete base if they are allowed to use a proprietary bonding paint on it, and it seems to work, even down to $\frac{3}{4}$ in/20 mm thickness which is about the minimum practicable, and this calls for considerable skill in avoiding over-trowelling which can cause cracking and dusting. The aggregates are usually required to be free from dust, but one specialist in granolithic floors calls for 10 per cent dust in the granite chippings. Sand must be clean, but the percentage of dust is very difficult to determine and from some pits and wet quarries may be non-existent. Washing may remove all dust which is not necessarily desirable.

All such pavings must be laid in bays which should enable good levels to be given but this is often very carelessly done, the undulations being detected underfoot better than by eye. Curing is strangely ignored, even by the application of a plastics spray seal, but draughts should certainly not be allowed; these are sometimes created to hasten drying.

Application of plastics-type tile or sheet flooring must await drying out of the screed, but the acceptable level of moisture content varies with the capacity of the material to breathe, enabling moisture vapour to escape instead of getting trapped. Where underfloor heating is installed a much drier screed is necessary, and a different kind of plastics-type tile adhesive which does not soften through heat should be used. All defects in the screed and in the spreading of adhesive show through plastics tile and sheet floorings, which is much too late to do remedial work. A roller is used to press the flooring down evenly but corners have a habit of lifting which can be dangerous to elderly people and so may require quicker attention than the normal defects liability period.

There are many kinds of masonry floorings, such as quarry tile, stone, marble, ceramic tile, mosaic and terrazzo, none of which can be finished well unless the screed base is good. All these are now regarded as suitable for specialist layers, and many of them require setting-out drawings, but some builders are well able to lay entirely satisfactory quarry tile floors and should be able to cope also with stone pavings.

Shrinkage cracking unfortunately affects most hard floorings but is catered for in terrazzo, mosaic and marble floorings but seldom in others, being defined by metal or plastics separation strip. The larger the area contained by separation strip the more likely cracking will occur in the space, so one is driven to having always smaller spaces.

Wood block paving or flooring used to be bedded in hot bitumen, which stuck it to the base and protected it from rising damp, but there was no control over moisture content. Now the screed must be thoroughly dry to prevent any moisture rising into the blocks, whose moisture content is often as low as 10 per cent, which is likely to be lower than the general level in the building. The result of swelling of wood blocks can be quite remarkable: partitions have been pushed out of place and even external walls damaged. Where expansion of the mass has been impossible, sudden upheavals of the flooring have occurred. It is not worth risking the laying of wood block flooring until the conditions are favourable.

Wood mosaic flooring does not appear to resent so much changes in moisture content, possibly because the pieces are small and the tiles are seldom tightly fitted.

One advantage of wood flooring over masonry floorings other than terrazzo is that they can be rubbed down by machine. There is not much scope for more than a superficial grinding off where wood mosaic flooring is concerned and where blocks are used some blocks have tongues or dowels to hold them in place which limit the amount of wear they afford but which may be much reduced by over-grinding where laid over a hump in the screed. Careless use of the sanding machine can damage skirtings badly.

Cork tile flooring is probably the easiest kind to lay and the least disposed to show defects in the base, but it is inclined to absorb moisture from above as well as below, causing swelling and lifting. This flooring is also probably the most difficult to keep clean and should be sealed by synthetic resin polish as soon as possible. This treatment is also recommended for wood floors of all kinds and is best done by the flooring specialists as they can keep other trades out until the sealer has dried. Other trades cannot be kept out indefinitely from all floored surfaces, but the architect should insist on hardboard protection being laid and kept in place, which ought of course to be a specification clause.

The extent to which an architect can supervise the formation of roads and paths together with drainage when he can only visit the site from time to time is questionable. There is much that can go wrong between visits. The setting out of roads on a large housing estate would be done piecemeal in detail but the base lines would be set out in one continuous operation, the node points being concreted in. Depending on the quality of the contractor, the extent to which this basic setting out should be checked by the architect is variable. It may need a survey party of four for the job and is largely repeating the original survey. It is possible that trigonometrical checking of the node points would be sufficient and could be much more accurate on a steeply sloping site than a chain survey. Checking in this manner would be a continuing process for, as the work proceeded, extensions from the base lines would be made which the architect ought to check at the periodic visits.

Many questions arise during inspections, among them whether the services crossing the roads should be laid before or after rolling of hardcore, whether a crossfall can be accepted where the roads turn with the contours and whether the gullies placed as shown on the drawing will catch the stormwater or not. Then there is the constant flow of indifferent hardcore and equally indifferent sorting and placing apart from identification of soft spots in the formation.

Mud and road constructions are almost inseparable, but mud in the hardcore, on the hardcore, in the carpeting and on the carpeting cannot be allowed, and this requires firm discipline to ensure. Hot asphalt surfacing is also a continuing process where every load ought to have its temperature checked before it is accepted to prove that it is neither too hot nor too cold. Thickness of carpet and wearing coat should be to Code of Practice but unless the architect is on the spot all the time how can he be sure? Responsible specialists fortunately do not give short measure.

Cold bitumen carpets require time for hardening, and so after rolling heavy traffic must be kept off for a time, which will depend on the weather conditions.

During the operations much rubbish will have fallen into the sumps of the road gullies and quite a lot of mud may have entered the drains. The gullies must be cleaned out and the drain lines seen to be clear of major obstructions, but it is not practicable to clear them of thin coatings of mud which in time will be flushed away by rain. Lumps of mud are another matter, but these will normally only be seen by sighting between manholes, those in the runs from gullies to manholes only being traceable by back rodding which is difficult to justify unless there is firm evidence of obstruction.

In the supervision of internal pavings, levels are most important, both as to height of base above datum and deviations from this within rooms. If an upper floor structural slab has its upper surface falling 1 in/25 mm between walls, should the cement and sand screed for vinyl flooring be laid to the specified thickness of $1\frac{1}{2}$ in/38 mm overall, or be as intended in the drawings $1\frac{1}{2}$ in/38 mm minimum and consequently $2\frac{1}{2}$ in/63 mm maximum; if the latter decision is made what have the structural engineer and the building inspector to say about the overloading result in the structural slab?

Screed for thin flexible floorings is very rarely as good as the architect would wish; it is virtually never so flat as similar floorings laid on hardboard. Unfortunately the poor quality of finish is seldom observable until after the sheet material has been laid, but it can be illuminating to test the surfaces with 6 ft/2 m long straight edges. Hollows of as much as $\frac{1}{8}$ in/3 mm are often found which would show very badly in the finished floor but might not show so badly if the finish were cork tile or wood block, for both can be sanded to remove the worst differences in level. This practice is obviously not good for the wearing thickness is thereby reduced. The alternative is to level out the screed with a rubber, bitumen or epoxy-resin mastic at considerable cost which the builder ought to bear, but he may claim that the architect is unreasonable in the standard of acceptance he has adopted. This standard may be affected by the quality of the job; an entrance hall having strong daylight at both ends presents the worst conditions when every sweep of the trowel on the screed seems to catch the light, but in houses the small rooms and large coverage by carpets and rugs hides a lot of faults.

Where wood block, wood mosaic and ceramic or masonry floorings are laid, there is the occasional hollow, loose or broken member to be looked for, and the unsanded upstanding edge. Sealing coats ought to be applied as soon as a surface is finished, and on wood in particular variations in absorbency often result in dull patches. These are not so much deficient in seal as in polish and so could be excused, but the floor is obviously not presenting the reflection all over that was intended so it should be given added treatment. Hollow sounding floorings may be found to be very little at fault, the hollow ring resulting from lack of adhesion to the bed much more than a measurable hollowness. If more cement bedding is then applied, the slab finishes too high; in fact it may be impossible to put it back to the correct level once disturbed, but the best hope would be to use some kind of fluid adhesive. Cracking of slab flooring sometimes results from shrinkage of the bed material, which is presumably due to too rich a mixture coupled with too much water. The overall cracking which resulted in one case fortunately had the appearance of being part of the pattern of the slabs.

If dusting of cement and sand or granolithic floorings develops during the defects liability period, the question to be answered is whether to require the builder to hack up and relay the floorings or to accept them but apply some kind of surface sealer. It is most unlikely that a client will agree to wholesale relaying of floorings in an occupied building, while he is quite likely to ask the architect why he did not so supervise the laying of the screed floorings as to ensure dusting did not develop. In one bad case the architect cross-examined the floor screeder to test his knowledge of good mixing and trowelling practice, his enthusiastic interest in his replies reassuring the architect; but these high principles went by the board when the layer decided he must finish the floor that evening, and he added so much water to the mix for the final stages to make spreading and levelling easier that, after hardening, a cloud of dust rose every time the final stage was brushed.

Non-acceptance of screed during the period of the contract may result in a delay in handover of several weeks. There is the time required for hacking up, then re-screeding, then drying out sufficiently to receive non-breathing finishes. The cost to a client of this protracted delay could run into thousands of pounds, for which the architect could be blamed on the argument that his specification was faulty, his selection of specialist layers was bad, his acceptance of structural slab as suitable for screed was wrong because of surface dirt and dust, his omission of a binding solution a contributory factor and his inadequate supervision a root cause. His main defence would appear to be that he was only required by the terms of his engagement to make periodic inspections, but there are so many holes in his defence that he might well feel his case lost.

# CHAPTER 17

# *Practical Completion*

The *form of contract* allows of partial completion where the client wishes to make use of one or a number of parts of a building contract. Each must then be usable to the extent that the client wishes, which may be before all services are functioning, as could be the case where machinery is to be installed in a dust-free atmosphere but cannot be used until services were available for the users. The extent to which a partial completion is to be taken should be agreed with the client before the contract is signed.

Clients may also wish to enter a building before the builders have finished all their work, but if this has not been a condition in the contract the builders could refuse entry. Or they might allow entry but ask for payment for disruption of their work due to special care having to be taken to protect the client's work and workpeople. This often happens when a contract period has expired and extension of time has not been allowed by the architect. Whether the builder should be compensated for disruption depends on the merits of the case. A particularly difficult situation arises where the client's workpeople cause damage to the building in entering before handing over, assigning blame being complicated by there being two bodies of workpeople in occupation.

One does not expect a building contract to be finished at practical completion, though in rare cases this may be the case. It may be finished to the extent that all trades believe they have done the works required of them, but it is only in the best managed contracts, by architects and builders, that the foremen for all trades check that there are no adjustments, easings, touchings-up, etc. which must be done before the handover meeting. This assumes that the foremen concerned are primarily tradesmen and know the standard of work required by their employers, which may not be the same as that expected by the architect. It is usual, then, if the client seriously intends to take possession of the whole or part of a building and its external works immediately after issue of a Certificate of Practical Completion, to make inspections a few days prior to the appointed date so that the builder, preferably accompanying the architect, can get the small remaining works done by that appointed date.

The architect should be well aware of which trades are least likely to be finished before making his inspection and should have been urging the builder to put pressure on the lagging trades, but whether the architect expects some trades to be unfinished or not, he should make his inspection in an orderly way and as far as possible without deviation from a set sequence. At an inspection prior to the appointed date it is not necessary for him to be accompanied by the builder's representative so long as the architect gives the builder a list of the items he has noticed to be incomplete in time to get the work done and discusses those which are least likely to be completed. The advantage of having the builder going round with him is that the builder may appreciate that some jobs unfinished are waiting for other trades which may be subcontractors so he has to chase them and not just his own staff.

At the inspection for practical completion the client may wish to be represented, which can be helpful or a nuisance—helpful if the representative can say that an unfinished job such as fixing non-illuminated signs can be left for a few days, but he might say that an incinerator must be fixed before he can accept a lavatory.

The inspection requires the architect to look at every trade but this is quite impossible, if only because scaffolding has been removed, but the time factor enters into the matter too. It is usual to start the inspection at the boundaries of the site, then roads and footpaths, lighting, stormwater and foul drainage, but not to the extent of applying further tests. It is as well, however, to have lightweight manhole covers lifted to see whether they have been painted on the underside and have been set in grease—this can be very annoying to the builder, for the grease, having been disturbed, has to be re-prepared before the covers are put back. Puddles in tar paving may not be evident, but this is not important at this stage as more puddles are likely to develop during the defects liability period, and only annoying puddles, such as those at entrance doors, need quick attention. Some external work may by agreement be unfinished, such as turfing, if the results would be better if left to later on.

After looking at external works the exterior of the building can be examined, but this should not occupy much time because periodic inspections should have covered all the defects, although there may be some brickwork to be cleaned down where splashing off scaffolding has marked it. There are balloons to look for on vent pipes and even falls to gutters which may have been shifted by ladders used after the scaffolding was removed. Binoculars are helpful sometimes, but detailed inspections at high level should not be necessary unless it is recalled that some correction was required which may not have been carried out—and if not should the correction be left until the end of the defects liability period?

Where flat roofs are concerned, if these can be reached from the interior it is probably better to defer inspection, but, if not, ladders must be called for and there one may find a surprising assortment of builder's rubbish—discarded sandwiches, displaced duckboards, missing balloons and unpainted metalwork.

If flat roofs have been deferred they should be the first parts to be looked at after entering the building, followed by access doors, hangings and fastenings, then stairs to the top storey looking in rigid sequence at ceiling, lighting, walls, skirtings, windows, window ledges, wall switches, socket outlets, floors, hangings, fastenings (both springbolt and locking bolt) for excessive play though attention may be deferred to later, and all the decorations applied to the various parts as inspected. Usually there is a fair amount of builder's rubbish left behind radiators, in cupboards and swept into corners, the difference between a builder's cleaning up and a 'cleaner's clean-up' being quite striking, though a good builder will often arrange for the final clean-up to be done by office cleaning contractors.

There is also the inspection of installations, but by this time the architect should have had some assurance from the specialists that their work is either complete or will be finished by the appointed date. The architect in going round may, however, in following his pre-arranged sequence of inspection items, find that adjustable louvres have not been set, or radiator wheel valves are left in various degrees of opening, that telephone jacks are missing, screws are missing from floor services coverplates and that floor tiles are still to be cut around pipes.

Unless this is written down in an orderly fashion it is not easy to copy or for another inspector to understand. It is not necessary to note that works are complete: only that they are incomplete and to what extent. The notes should be permanent records so the first sheet would give the name of the job and job number together with date of inspection and names of those making the inspection. The subtitle would note which part was being inspected, *e.g.*: *external works*: Boundary fences and gates, etc., then *buildings*: *externally* followed in time by *buildings*: *internally* followed by identification of part such as *block A*. In the stairways the identity of each stair would be given separately such as *stair A* followed by *roof level* then the notes of defects to ceilings, ceiling lighting fittings, then wall defects, door and ironmongery defects, but probably set out with margins, the left one for filing and the right hand one for comments such as 'defer', or 'urgent' or maybe 'chase PO'. All the works listed have to be attended to, but some are more important than others or are likely to take longer.

Typing time can be saved by using a carbon paper duplicate book, or preferably a triplicate book if the architect's writing can be deciphered without much difficulty. Some architects prefer to go round with the builder's representative and get him to make notes of the jobs to be attended to. This is not a good practice, for the architect has no means of knowing what items he has noticed and even if the builder gives him a copy there is no proof that some items have not been left off, not necessarily deliberately but because in talking about the items discussion left no time for scribbling them down. The inspection for handing over is not an examination for defects such as is made at the end of the defects liability period, though there may be some items which if not corrected could prevent occupation. The architect should for example have checked that all WWPs flush easily and refill reasonably rapidly, and that all compartment door locks function easily so he should not have to do this again at an inspection for practical completion but in passing a drinking fountain he might satisfy himself with a quick push on the lever that the control valve has been adjusted since his last visit so that use of the lever did not result in mains pressure water sending a shower all over the lavatory. The observant architect with a good memory can quickly make an effective inspection-cum-examination.

If there is doubt about the building being ready for possession on the appointed date, the architect should inform the client, for he may be aware of this possibility and have limited his plans to having carpets laid and lighting fittings put up, but if this is the case the architect must ensure that the builder cleans floors thoroughly, dirty floors being one of the items which seem to annoy clients more than unfinished decorations.

When the contract is running late, the builder may make strenuous efforts to get it in a fit state for handing over, especially if there is a penalty clause which could be invoked. He may then try to persuade the architect that the unfinished jobs can be done after the building has been handed over. Retail shops which have advertised their opening dates would be very reluctant to have builder's workpeople coming in and might say they will not permit any work to be done after their opening date. Office users and householders are much more amenable, but may demand that the builders should ensure completion of certain parts, such as reception area, kitchen and sanitary accommodation. The builder is entitled to part of the retention sum on practical completion, so a difficult situation arises when he fails to complete but the client takes possession and refuses to let the builder enter. The value of work unfinished is probably small but the discomfort to the client may be considerable, and the issue by the architect of a certificate releasing half the retention sum could produce a sharp response unfavourable to the architect and builder. Release of this money is of course necessary not only for the builder but for the subcontractors too, so it is likely the architect would have to negotiate with the client for release of a sum which would enable the subcontractors to be paid, but which might penalise to some extent the builder who might have to be persuaded by the architect that this was the easiest way. The builder would of course object that this was unfair in that, if he had been allowed to enter after the client had taken possession, he could have completed all the jobs within a week or thereabouts, which could be true, but non-completion was the builder's fault so he must suffer for it.

The *Form of Contract* requires the builder to attend to defects during the period of defects liability, but the intention was probably to safeguard the client's interests in that in previous forms the builder could defer attention to defects until the end of the period. A pipe which sprang a leak at a joint just after practical completion could in theory have been left to leak for months but this is not so now.

A certificate of practical completion unaccompanied by a schedule of unfinished works indicates a very satisfactory state of affairs. Where a schedule of unfinished works must be attached, there should be agreement with the client as to when these are to be attended to, *i.e.* as soon as the client can allow the builder to do them, during a works holiday shut-down or after the end of the defects liability period. Some of them which at the inspection seemed unimportant may during the period develop an urgency demanding quick action, but this situation would be covered by terms of the contract. It is necessary of course that the architect should know of this so that the item may be struck off the schedule. Should the architect inspect such work affecting completion during the period of liability? It could mean travelling time and inconvenience. If it was a job that required opening up, doing the work and re-instating covering, he ought to but a complacent client who knows what he is about might agree to pass the work on the architect's behalf, for which no doubt the architect would be truly grateful. The architect would be well advised to discuss the work with the client later to satisfy himself that the builder co-operated well and that the client was content.

# CHAPTER 18

# *Final Completion*

The architect is required to issue a list of defects at the end of the defects liability period within a certain time, at present 14 days. On large contracts there may be so many defects that there is not enough time to make elaborate inspections and have them typed and sent to the builders, so it is often necessary to commence the inspections before the end of the period. It is therefore desirable to enter in the diary not only the date of the end of the liability period but a reminder some days ahead, for apart from the architect's own organisation the builder's organisation could also be affected if he wants to be represented.

At practical completion or when the client takes possession it is normal to remind him that a further inspection will be made at the end of the liability period and ask him to make a list of items which come to light during the period which require the builder's attention, additional to those on the schedule attached to the practical completion certificate. Department heads in large buildings would probably be asked to make their own lists, and no doubt some may regard this as an impertinence for the architect is paid to do this work—so why should someone else do it for him? This attitude is human but unhelpful, but it is possible the architect's approach might be to ask whether any points have been noticed rather than to ask for a list.

In addition to the builder's work there is of course the specialist's work to be checked, some of which the architect must assume to be correct unless he is told it is not. Malfunctioning of installations usually produces a strong response in clients, which the architect quickly hears about and gets action taken by the responsible installer during the liability period, so by the time the period is ended teething troubles have been ironed out.

Joint inspections by architect and builder's representative are desirable even though much argument may result. A crack through a lightweight concrete block partition may be due to excessive length without a shrinkage joint which the architect forgot to specify and which should now be formed, for which the builder should be paid. Puddles in roads and paths are likely to be due to insufficient consolidation of hardcore, but the builder may point out that some puddles occur over a trench cut after the road was hardcored and the backfill could not be consolidated equal to the general hardcore because the architect would not authorise concrete casing to the service or backfill in weak concrete. Or it might turn out that the client had tapped off an underground service during the period and had had a good patch repair done to tarmac but not to formation. Where a plasterboard ceiling has been skimmed and hair cracks have occurred at the joints in the boards, the builder may say this is to be expected and the cracks are not defects for the purpose of the contract. The architect probably knows that this is true and he might agree to that extent with the builder, but he should point out that the builder knew when tendered that this was the ceiling finish and that hair cracking would result, so he should have made provision in his rates for making good the cracks and re-decorating the ceilings —in fact redecoration with emulsion paint will probably be sufficient to fill the cracks. To re-decorate every such ceiling could be a very expensive item for the builder, but unless stopping every crack is done, the defects remain and the architect must decide whether to accept the defects or get them put right.

Shrinkage of joinery timber is a common source of disagreement. Some joinery must be brought on site before heating is available so shrinkage to a perceptible degree must be expected. Other joinery may be held back until after heating has been started, but before the plaster and floor screed have thoroughly dried out, and so the joinery may have absorbed moisture and then given it up again, with results that may show in the finished work.

The architect is often in a dilemma, but he must make up his mind at the inspection while listening to the counter arguments of the builder. It may be that later consideration and discussion will decide him to change his decision even if this is after the schedule has been sent to the builder.

The architect may also find himself at loggerheads with his client who expected some work to be done in a different way from what was effected. The cause of this will normally be inadequate briefing by the client, and the builder should not be expected to pay the cost of re-doing the work to the client's satisfaction.

The preparation of the schedule would follow exactly the same lines as the inspection for practical completion, but it must be much more thorough and unequivocal. The notes should be filed after copying, the builder being sent at least two copies and the quantity surveyors one copy, for quite a number of the items in the schedule may be additional works which the quantity surveyor must value, with another copy to the clerk of works, if any. Whether the client should have a copy is questionable; it may depend upon how much disruption will be caused by the builder's entry and on phasing access to the builder's site with process sequences. It may be sufficient to indicate to the client what parts are affected and if possible how long the work will take.

The programme for attending to defects is commonly impossible to extract from a builder. He has by this time had most of his money and he makes no profit on attending to defects. He can employ his labour much more profitably on new contracts, and moreover his men are not keen on working on these fiddling defects when they could be earning a good bonus elsewhere. The work will probably get done as each trade finishes more interesting and pressing work elsewhere, so the architect is often harried by the client to get the builder to finish off, and he in turn pleads with the builder to get shot of the job, but he really has little influence on him. It is rare to find a builder who shares the architect's view that the quicker the job is finished the better for all concerned, but the risk then is that the defects will be badly attended to and may have to be re-done more than once before the architect is satisfied—if he ever is. On very small jobs the builders have just not bothered to return to the site or to claim the balance of the contract sum, knowing that there is nothing worth while the architect or client can do to compel his attendance and satisfactory performance.

It follows that the certificate of final completion may have to be issued with less than complete satisfaction, so where the architect has a builder who conscientiously does all that is expected of him he is unusually favoured. Fortunately there are in fact many builders, of small and large organisations, who take a pride in their good organisation, efficient staffs and able workpeople, with whose work the architect has good reason to be satisfied.

With the issue of the certificate of final completion should also go to the client copies of the drawings 'as built', but more often these follow after some delay, although they certainly ought to be sent before the final payment is made on certificate, otherwise there is a real risk that they will never be sent at all. The client can of course deal with this by withholding payment of the balance of fees and expenses due to the architect.

# Index

183

Trial holes, 32, 38
Trial panels, 64, 70

Vandalism, 20
Vapour barriers, 5, 113, 132, 138
Variations, 14, 15
  recording, 15
VDPC, *see* Vertical dampproof
  course
Veneers, 95, 96
Vertical dampproof course (VDPC),
  7
Vibrators, 50
Visits
  special, 2
  frequency, 2

Wall papering, 161
  colour/pattern matching, 162, 164
  defects, 163
  pastes, 162
  staining, 163
Wall ties, 65
Wall tiling, 152

Waste systems, 123
Water authorities, 47, 117
Water/cement ratio, 50, 51
Water installations
  testing, 123
  insulation, 125
  materials, 119, 121
  protection, 119, 120
  sterilisation, 122
  warning pipes, 118, 120
Water meters, 118
Water percolation, 42
Weather, wet, 36
Weatherboarding, 82, 98
Welfare, 27
Well points, 40
Wind pressure, 75, 105
Wind suction, 75, 105, 110
Windows
  damage to, 76
  danger from, 76
  fittings, 76
Wood priming, 127

Zinc, 72, 102